EVIDENCE OF TRADITION

EVIDENCE OF TRADITION

SELECTED SOURCE MATERIAL
FOR THE STUDY OF THE HISTORY OF
THE EARLY CHURCH
THE NEW TESTAMENT BOOKS
THE NEW TESTAMENT CANON

BY
DANIEL J. THERON
M.A., Th. D.

WIPF & STOCK · Eugene, Oregon

Wipf and Stock Publishers
199 W 8th Ave, Suite 3
Eugene, OR 97401

Evidence of Tradition
Selected Source Material for the Study of the History of the
Early Church the New Testament Books and the New Testament Canon
By Theron, Daniel J.
ISBN 13: 978-1-60608-588-2
Publication date 4/8/2009
Previously published by Baker Book House, 1957

CONTENTS

Preface	xi
The Most Important Abbreviations	xiii
Signs	xiii
Introductory Remarks	xiv

I. HISTORY

Literature on Judaism	1
General Literature	1

A. Jewish Sources

1	Josephus, *Ant.*, xviii.3.3	4
2	*Ant.*, xx.9.1	4
3	*Ant.*, xviii.5.2	6
4	Origen, *Against Celsus*, i.47	6
5	Slavonic Addition to the *Jewish War*	9

B. Gentile Sources

6	Tacitus, *Ann.*, xv.44.2	10
7	Suetonius, *Claud.*, xxv	12
8	*Nero*, xvi	12
9	Pliny to Trajan; Trajan to Pliny, *Letters*, x. xcvi–xcvii	12
10	Hadrian's Rescript to Minucius Fundanus, cf. Justin, *Apology*, 68.6	18
11	Epictetus, *Discourses*, iv.7.5–6	18
12	Mara, the Son of Serapion, to his Son, Serapion	21
13	The Inscription of Tibur	20
14	Gallio Inscription	22

C. Christian Sources

15	Letter of Abgar to Jesus	22
	Reply of Jesus to Abgar, cf. Eusebius, *C. H.*, i.13.6–10	24
16	Irenaeus, *Against Heresies*, ii.22.5	24
17	Irenaeus to Florinus, cf. Eusebius, *C. H.*, v.20.48	24
18	Papias, cf. Eusebius, *C. H.*, iii.39.1–7	26
19	cf. Codex Baroccianus, 142	30
20	cf. Codex Coislinianus, 305	30
21	Polycrates, cf. Eusebius, *C. H.*, iii.31.3	32
22	Argument, Vatic. Alex. no. 14	32

C. Christian Sources—(continued)

23 Origen, *Commentary on Matthew*, xvi.6	32
24 Syriac Martyrology	34
25 Clement of Rome, *To the Corinthians*, v.5–7	34
26 Description of Paul, *Acts of Paul and Thecla*, 3	34
27 Gaius, cf. Eusebius, *C. H.*, iii.28.1–2	36

II. HISTORY OF THE NEW TESTAMENT BOOKS

Literature .. 39

A. The Four Gospels

1. *Tatian*

28 Tatian, cf. Eusebius, *C. H.*, iv.29.6	40
29 Fragment	40

2. *Greek and Latin Fathers*

30 Irenaeus, *Against Heresies*, iii.1.1–2	42
31 Clement of Alexandria, *Outlines*, cf. Eusebius, *C. H.*, vi.14.5	44
32 Tertullian, *Against Marcion*, iv.2	44
33 iv.5	46
34 Eusebius, *C. H.*, iii.24.5–15	46
35 Jerome, Prologues to the four Gospels from his *Commentary on Matthew*	50
36 Matthew	52
37 Mark	52
38 Luke	52
39 John	52
40 Augustin, *The Harmony of the Gospels*, i.2.4	54

3. *Monarchian Prologues*

41 Argument of the Gospel according to Matthew	56
42 Argument of the Gospel according to John	58
43 Argument of the Gospel according to Luke	60
44 Argument of the Gospel according to Mark	62

B. The Gospel of Matthew

45 Papias, cf. Eusebius, *C. H.*, iii.39.16	64
46 Pantaenus of Alexandria, cf. Eusebius, *C. H.*, v.10.3	64
47 Jerome, *Illustrious Men*, iii	66

C. The Gospel of Mark

48 Papias, cf. Eusebius, *C. H.*, iii.39.15	66
49 Jerome, *Illustrious Men*, viii	66

Contents

D. The Gospel of Luke

50	Eusebius, *C. H.*, iii.4.6	68
51	Jerome, *Illustrious Men*, vii	70

E. The Gospel of John

52	Theophilus, *To Autolycus*, ii.22	72
53	Irenaeus, *Against Heresies*, iii.11.7	72
54	Jerome, *Illustrious Men*, ix	74
55	Fragment from the John Rylands Library	76

F. The Acts of the Apostles

56	Irenaeus, *Against Heresies*, iii.14.1	76
57	Clement of Alexandria, *Miscellanies*, v.82.4	78

G. Paul's Epistles

Marcionite Prologues

58	Romans	78
59	I Corinthians	78
60	II Corinthians	78
61	Galatians	80
62	Ephesians	80
63	Philippians	80
64	Colossians	80
65	I Thessalonians	80
66	II Thessalonians	82
67	I Timothy	82
68	II Timothy	82
69	Titus	82
70	Philemon	82

H. Hebrews

71	Clement of Alexandria, cf. Eusebius, *C. H.*, vi.13.6	84
72	cf. Eusebius, *C. H.*, vi.14.2–4	84
73	Origen, cf. Eusebius, *C. H.*, vi.25.11–14	84
74	Tertullian, *On Modesty*, xx	86

I. The Catholic Epistles

75	Clement of Alexandria, cf. Eusebius, *C. H.*, vi.14.1	88
76	Prologue to the Catholic Epistles	88

J. The Apocalypse

77	Justin Martyr, *Dialogue*, lxxxi.4	88
78	Hippolytus, *On the Antichrist*, xxv–xxvi	90

III. CANON

Literature 93

1. THE ENDING OF MARK

79 The Freer Logion, Freer MS.(W) 94
80 Jerome, *Against the Pelagians*, ii.15 94
81 The Short Ending of Mark, MSS. L and others .. 96

2. AGRAPHA

82 Acts 20.35 96
83 Oxyrhynchus Papyri, Second Saying 96
84   Fourth Saying 96
85 *The Teaching of the Twelve Apostles*, i.2.. 98
86 *Clementine Homilies*, xix.20 98
87 *Didascalia*, ii.3 98
88 Barnabas, vi.13 98

3. APOCRYPHAL AND CANONICAL GOSPELS

89 *The Gospel of Peter* 98
90 Origen, *Commentary on John*, ii.87 102
91 Jerome, *Against the Pelagians*, iii.2 102
92   *Commentary on Isaiah*, xi.2 104
93   *Illustrious Men*, II 104
94 Irenaeus, *Against Heresies*, i.3.6 106
95   iii.11.8 106

4. CANONICAL LISTS

96 The Muratorian Canon 106
97 Origen, cf. Eusebius, *C. H.*, vi.25.3–10 112
98 Eusebius, *C. H.*, iii.25 114
99 Cyrillus of Jerusalem, *Instruction*, iv.36 116
100 Athanasius, *39th Easter Letter*, 7–9, 11–12 118
101 Epiphanius, *Against Eighty Heresies*, iii. i. lxxvi.5 .. 118
102 Canon of Mommsen 120
103 Codex Sinaiticus 123
104 Codex Claromontanus 122
105 Canon of the Synod of Laodicea 124
106 Canon of the Synod of Carthage 126

APPENDICES

I. Roman Emperors 128
II. Legates of Syria 128
III. Procurators of Palestine 128
IV. The Herodians 129
V. Early Authors and Literature 129
    Index 131

PREFACE

The purpose of this book is to collect in one volume a number of sources which are significant for New Testament studies. By rendering these with translations those still unacquainted with Greek and Latin have access to source material. Further, the purpose is to stimulate, with the aid of the given material and suggested literature, the research of the student in the era of the early centuries when most of the traditions regarding the New Testament and its books received their ultimate characterization.

Tribute must be paid to the late William P. Armstrong of Princeton, New Jersey, whom the present author did not have the privilege to know in person. He acquired, or made translations for the some forty selections contained in his booklet, *Texts for Gospel History*, which was printed by The Princeton University Press in 1930, but he did not publish them. The fruit of his work was consulted by the present author in making the translations for the present volume containing one hundred and six selections.

The author wishes to express his sincere gratitude to Dr. Otto A. Piper of Princeton, New Jersey, for both advice and encouragement in this undertaking. The author also wishes to express his indebtedness to publishers who gave kind permission to quote from their works and to a few friends who made valuable contributions in the preparation and proof reading of this volume. In this respect he desires to make special mention of Dr. C. Wayland James of Easton Pennsylvania, Dr. Walter J. G. Hards, and the Rev. Philip A. Quanbeck of Princeton, New Jersey. Yet, they are in no wise responsible for any shortcomings that may be found in the work.

Princeton, New Jersey   DANIEL J. THERON
February 1955

NOTES

THE MOST IMPORTANT ABBREVIATIONS

General

adu.—*aduersus*
al.—*alii*
c.—*circa*
cf.—compare

ed.—edited
MS(S).—manuscript(s)
saec.—*saeculum*
s. u.—*sub uoce*

Titles

Adu. haer.—*Aduersus haereses*
Adu. Pelag.—*Aduersus Pelagianos*
Ann.—*Annales*
Ant.—*Antiquites*
Ap.—Appendix
A. V.—Authorized Version
C. Cel.—*Contra Celsum*
C. H.—Church History
C. I. L.—*Corpus Inscriptionum Latinarum*
Claud.—*Claudius*
C. Marc.—*Contra Marcionem*
De praescr. haer.—*De praescriptione haereticorum*
De uir. inl.—*De uiris inlustribus*
H. E.—*Historia ecclesiastica*
Hyp.—*Hypotyposes*
In Iohan.—*In Iohannem*
In Is.—*In Isaiam*
Rev. Bénéd.—*Revue Bénédictine*
T. u. U.—*Texte und Untersuchungen*
W.—Washingtonianus (Freer MS.)
ZNTW.—*Zeitschrift für die neutestamentliche Wissenschaft*

SIGNS

Square brackets [ ] in the Greek and Latin texts indicate a lacuna; in the translations and elsewhere they indicate words which were added for the sake of clarity.

Square brackets and two crosses [××] indicate that the word or words within them are mistaken additions.

Angular brackets ⟨ ⟩ in the Greek and Latin texts indicate a mistaken omission by the original scribe.

A dot under a letter — ạ β̣ etc. — in the Greek text indicates that it is doubtful.

Round brackets ( ) are used in the translations for brief explanations.

Quotation marks " ", when not used in the ordinary way, indicate that the one or at the most two words within them render the original text approximately.

A question mark within round brackets (?) indicates that the immediately preceding is uncertain.

Italics in the translations—*abcd* etc.—when not the title of a work, constitute the words entirely or partly preserved in an otherwise mutilated, original text.

INTRODUCTORY REMARKS

In translating the selections in this book it has been the author's aim to remain rather literal and, insofar as possible, to give account of every word of the original text.

When reference is made to an author for the first time his name is followed by dates indicating either the entire span of his life or the approximate period when he flourished. For the purpose of reference these data are repeated in Appendix V.

Due to the nature of the material the different chapters and their subdivisions could not be absolute. Because of this the Index should be consulted to obtain more complete information on subjects for which this volume might be used.

The texts, unless otherwise stated, were obtained from standard editions.

The literature given at the beginning of each chapter, or at the end of a selection, is merely by way of introduction and by far not complete. The tables of content and the indices of these books should be consulted. It was deemed unnecessary to refer to articles which are contained in standard dictionaries and encyclopaedias, since these are easily obtainable by regular methods. For a list of such dictionaries and encyclopaedias cf. Bruce M. Metzger, *A Guide to the Preparation of a Thesis* (*Princeton Pamphlets*, 4) (Princeton, 1950), pp. 6-8.

I. HISTORY

LITERATURE ON JUDAISM

Wilhelm Bousset, *Die Religion des Judentums im späthellenistischen Zeitalter*, 3. verbesserte Auflage, herausgegeben von Hugo Gressmann (*Handbuch zum Neuen Testament*, herausgegeben von Hans Lietzmann, 21), Tübingen, 1926.
Ch. Guignebert, *Le Monde Juif vers le temps de Jésus*, Paris, 1935. English translation by S. H. Hooke, *The Jewish World in the Time of Jesus*, London, 1939.
R. Travers Herford, *Christianity in Talmud and Midrash*, London, 1903.
George Foot Moore, *Judaism in the First Centuries of the Christian Era the Age of the Tannaim*, 3 vols., Cambridge (Mass.), 1932–1940.
Emil Schürer, *Geschichte der jüdischen Volkes im Zeitalter Jesu Christi*, 4. Auflage, 3 Bände. 1901–1907; Register, 1911. English translation from the 2nd edition, *A History of the Jewish People in the Time of Jesus Christ*, 3 vols., Edinburgh, 1885–1890; Index, 1891.

GENERAL LITERATURE

Otto Bardenhewer, *Geschichte der altkirchlichen Literatur*, 5 Bände, Freiburg, 1913–1932.
Henry Bettenson, *Documents of the Christian Church*, New York, 1947.
Clarence Tucker Craig, *The Beginning of Christianity*, New York and Nashville (Copyright, 1943).
Morton Scott Enslin, *Christian Beginnings*, New York and London, 1938.
F. J. Foakes-Jackson, Kirsopp Lake et al., *Beginnings of Christianity*, 5 vols., London, 1922–1942.
Edgar J. Goodspeed, *A History of Early Christian Literature*, Chicago, 1941.
Adolf von Harnack, *Die Mission und Ausbreitung des Christentums in den ersten drei Jahrhunderten*, 4. neu durchgearbeitete Auflage, 2 Bänden, Leipzig, 1923–1924. English translation by James Moffatt, *The Mission and Expansion of Early Christianity*, 2 vols., New York and London, 1905.

———, *Geschichte der altchristlichen Litteratur bis Eusebius. Die Chronologie*, 2 Bände, Leipzig, 1897-1904.
H. Jordan, *Geschichte der altchristlichen Literatur*, Leipzig, 1911.
Julius Lebreton and Jacques Zeiller, *The History of the Primitive Church*, 2 vols., New York, 1949.
Hans Lietzmann, *Geschichte der Alten Kirchen*, 3 Bände, Berlin und Leipzig, 1932-1938. English translation by B. L. Woolf, *The Beginnings of the Christian Church*, 2 vols., New York, 1937.
Alfred Loisy, *La naissance du Christianisme*, Paris, 1933.
James MacKinnon, *From Christ to Constantine, The Rise and Growth of the Early Church (c. A. D. 30 to 337)*, London and New York, 1936.
Eduard Meyer, *Ursprung und Anfänge des Christentums*, 3 Bände, Stuttgart und Berlin, 1921-1923.
James Moffatt, *The First Five Centuries of the Church* (*The London Theological Library*), New York and Nashville, 1938 (N. B. pp. 211-247 for bibliography).
Jacques Moreau, *Les plus anciens témoignages profanes sur Jésus* (*Collection lebèque*, 5me Série—No. 51), Bruxelles, 1944.
Robert Rainy, *The Ancient Catholic Church from the Accession of Trajan to the Fourth General Council (A. D. 98-451)*, New York, 1902.
W. M. Ramsay, *The Church in the Roman Empire before A. D. 170*, New York and London, 1893.
Burnett Hillman Streeter, *The Primitive Church, Studied with Special Reference to the Origins of the Christian Ministry. Lectures delivered on the Hewett Foundation*, New York, 1929.
Studies and Documents, ed. Kirsopp and Silva Lake, 15 parts, ff., London, 1934-1947 ff.
Texte und Untersuchungen zur Geschichte der altchristlichen Literatur, herausgegeben von Oscar von Gebhardt und Adolf von Harnack, 15 Bände, Leipzig, 1882-1896; *Texte und Untersuchungen zur Geschichte der altchristlichen Literatur*, neue Folge, Leipzig, 1897ff.
Johannes Weiss und Rudolf Knopf, *Das Urchristentum*, Göttingen, 1914-1917. English translation ed. by Frederick C. Grant, *The History of Primitive Christianity*, New York, 1937.

Iosephus

1

Γίνεται δὲ κατὰ τοῦτον τὸν χρόνον Ἰησοῦς σοφὸς ἀνήρ, εἴγε ἄνδρα αὐτὸν λέγειν χρή· ἦν γὰρ παραδόξων ἔργων ποιητής, διδάσκαλος ἀνθρώπων τῶν ἡδονῇ τἀληθῆ δεχομένων, καὶ πολλοὺς μὲν Ἰουδαίους, πολλοὺς δὲ καὶ τοῦ Ἑλληνικοῦ ἐπηγάγετο· ὁ χριστὸς οὗτος ἦν. καὶ αὐτὸν ἐνδείξει τῶν πρώτων ἀνδρῶν παρ' ἡμῖν σταυρῷ ἐπιτετιμηκότος Πιλάτου οὐκ ἐπαύσαντο οἱ τὸ πρῶτον ἀγαπήσαντες· ἐφάνη γὰρ αὐτοῖς τρίτην ἔχων ἡμέραν πάλιν ζῶν τῶν θείων προφητῶν ταῦτά τε καὶ ἄλλα μυρία περὶ αὐτοῦ θαυμάσια εἰρηκότων. εἰς ἔτι τε νῦν τῶν Χριστιανῶν ἀπὸ τοῦδε ὠνομασμένον οὐκ ἐπέλιπε τὸ φῦλον.

Iosephus *Ant.* XVIII.3.3(63), cf. Eusebius *H.E.* I.11.7.

2

Ἅτε δὴ οὖν τοιοῦτος ὢν ὁ Ἄνανος, νομίσας ἔχειν καιρὸν ἐπιτήδειον διὰ τὸ τεθνάναι μὲν Φῆστον, Ἀλβῖνον δ' ἔτι κατὰ τὴν ὁδὸν ὑπάρχειν, καθίζει συνέδριον κριτῶν καὶ παραγαγὼν εἰς αὐτὸ τὸν ἀδελφὸν Ἰησοῦ τοῦ λεγομένου Χριστοῦ, Ἰάκωβος ὄνομα αὐτῷ, καί τινας ἑτέρους, ὡς παρανομησάντων κατηγορίαν ποιησάμενος παρέδωκε λευσθησομένους. ὅσοι δὲ ἐδόκουν ἐπιεικέστατοι τῶν κατὰ τὴν πόλιν εἶναι καὶ περὶ τοὺς νόμους ἀκριβεῖς βαρέως ἤνεγκαν ἐπὶ τούτῳ καὶ πέμπουσιν πρὸς τὸν βασιλέα κρύφα παρακαλοῦντες αὐτὸν ἐπιστεῖλαι τῷ Ἀνάνῳ μηκέτι τοιαῦτα πράσσειν· μηδὲ γὰρ τὸ πρῶτον ὀρθῶς αὐτὸν πεποιηκέναι.

Iosephus *Ant.* XX.9.1(200), cf. Eusebius *H.E.* II.1.4; II.23.4; II.23.20.

A. Jewish Sources

JOSEPHUS (A.D. 37-c. 95)

1

There was about this time[1] Jesus, a wise man, if indeed it be right to call him a man; for he was a doer of marvellous works, a teacher of men who received the truth with pleasure; and he won over to himself many Jews and many of the Greek [race] also. This one was the Christ. And when, upon accusation of the leading men among us, Pilate had condemned him to [the] cross, those who had loved [him] at the first did not cease; for he appeared to them alive again on [the] third day, as the divine prophets had spoken these and ten thousand other wonderful things concerning him. And even until now the "sect" of Christians, named after this one, has not ceased.

[1]During the administration of Pilate.

2

Ananus being such an one,[1] [and] thinking that he had a convenient opportunity because Festus had died[2] and Albinus was still on the way, assembled [the] Sanhedrin of judges and, bringing into it the brother of Jesus, who was called the Christ— James was his name—and certain others, and having made an accusation [against them] as transgressors of the law, he delivered [them] to be stoned. But those in the city who seemed to be the most moderate and careful about [the observance of] the laws were indignant at this and sent secretly to the king[3] urging him to write to Ananus not to do such things; for [they thought] that he had not done what was right in the first instance.

[1]Described in the context as "bold, ruthless and a Sadducee."
[2]Festus died in A.D. 62 and Albinus was sent from Rome as his successor.
[3]Herod Agrippa II.

3

Τισὶ δὲ τῶν Ἰουδαίων ἐδόκει ὀλωλέναι τὸν Ἡρώδου στρατὸν ὑπὸ τοῦ θεοῦ καὶ μάλα δικαίως τινυμένου κατὰ ποινὴν Ἰωάννου τοῦ ἐπικαλουμένου βαπτιστοῦ. κτείνει γὰρ δὴ τοῦτον Ἡρώδης ἀγαθὸν ἄνδρα καὶ τοῖς Ἰουδαίοις κελεύοντα ἀρετὴν ἐπασκοῦσιν καὶ τὰ πρὸς ἀλλήλους δικαιοσύνῃ καὶ πρὸς τὸν θεὸν εὐσεβείᾳ χρωμένοις βαπτισμῷ συνιέναι· οὕτω γὰρ δὴ καὶ τὴν βάπτισιν ἀποδεκτὴν αὐτῷ φανεῖσθαι μὴ ἐπί τινων ἁμαρτάδων παραιτήσει χρωμένων, ἀλλ' ἐφ' ἁγνείᾳ τοῦ σώματος, ἅτε δὴ καὶ τῆς ψυχῆς δικαιοσύνῃ προεκκεκαθαρμένης. καὶ τῶν ἀνθρώπων συστρεφομένων, καὶ γὰρ ἤσθησαν ἐπὶ πλεῖστον τῇ ἀκροάσει τῶν λόγων, δείσας Ἡρώδης τὸ ἐπὶ τοσόνδε πιθανὸν αὐτοῦ τοῖς ἀνθρώποις μὴ ἐπὶ ἀποστάσει τινὶ φέροι, πάντα γὰρ ἐῴκεσαν συμβουλῇ τῇ ἐκείνου πράξοντες, πολὺ κρεῖττον ἡγεῖται πρίν τι νεώτερον ἐξ αὐτοῦ γενέσθαι προλαβὼν ἀνελεῖν τοῦ μεταβολῆς γενομένης εἰς πράγματα ἐμπεσὼν μετανοεῖν. καὶ ὁ μὲν ὑποψίᾳ τῇ Ἡρώδου δέσμιος εἰς τὸν Μαχαιροῦντα πεμφθεὶς τὸ προειρημένον φρούριον ταύτῃ κτίννυται. τοῖς δὲ Ἰουδαίοις δόξα ἦν ἐπὶ τιμωρίᾳ τῇ ἐκείνου τὸν ὄλεθρον ἐπὶ τῷ στρατεύματι γενέσθαι τοῦ θεοῦ κακῶσαι Ἡρώδην θέλοντος.

Iosephus *Ant.* XVIII.5.2(116), cf. Eusebius *H.E.* I.11.4.

Origen de Iosepho

4

Ὁ Ἰώσηπος μαρτυρεῖ τῷ Ἰωάννῃ ὡς βαπτιστῇ γεγενημένῳ καὶ καθάρσιον τοῖς βαπτισμένοις ἐπαγγελλομένῳ. ὁ δ' αὐτὸς καίτοι γε ἀπιστῶν τῷ Ἰησοῦ ὡς χριστῷ, ζητῶν τὴν αἰτίαν τῆς τῶν Ἱεροσολύμων πτώσεως καὶ τῆς τοῦ ναοῦ καθαιρέσεως, δέον αὐτὸν εἰπεῖν ὅτι ἡ κατὰ τοῦ Ἰησοῦ ἐπιβουλὴ τούτων αἰτία γέγονε τῷ λαῷ, ἐπεὶ ἀπέκτειναν τὸν προφητευόμενον χριστόν· ὁ δὲ καὶ ὥσπερ ἄκων οὐ μακρὰν τῆς ἀληθείας γενόμενός φησι ταῦτα συμβεβηκέναι τοῖς Ἰουδαίοις κατ' ἐκδίκησιν Ἰακώβου τοῦ δικαίου, ὃς ἦν ἀδελφὸς Ἰησοῦ τοῦ λεγομένου χριστοῦ, ἐπειδήπερ δικαιότατον αὐτὸν ὄντα ἀπέκτειναν.

Origen *C. Cel.* I.47.

3

But to certain of the Jews it seemed that the army of Herod[1] had been destroyed[2] by God, quite justly indeed, punishing him in retribution for John, who was called the Baptist. For Herod killed this one, a good man and one who commanded the Jews, who practiced virtue and applied justice in matters pertaining to one another and [showed] piety toward God, to come together for baptism. For thus would the baptism appear acceptable to Him, if they made use of it, not to seek remission of certain sins, but for the purification of the body seeing that the soul had before been cleansed by righteousness. And when the people were gathering together—for indeed they took very great pleasure in listening to his words—Herod, fearing his great influence over the people lest it should lead to some revolt—for they seemed likely to follow his advice in all things—thought it very much better, intervening before any revolutionary movement should spring up from him, to put him to death rather than, falling into difficulties after an insurrection had occurred, to repent [of his failure to intervene]. And, because of the suspicion of Herod, he was sent [as] a prisoner to Machaerus, the above mentioned fortress, [and] was put to death there. But to the Jews it seemed that destruction befell the army as punishment for that [man], since God had determined to punish Herod.

[1]Herod Antipas, Tetrarch of Galilee and Perea, 4 B. C.–A. D. 39.
[2]By Aretas, king of the Nabataeans, *c.* A. D. 36.

ORIGEN ON JOSEPHUS
(A.D. *c.* 182/186–251/254)

4

Josephus testifies to John as having become a baptist and as promising purification to those who were baptized. But he, although himself not believing in Jesus as Christ, seeking the cause of the fall of Jerusalem and of the destruction of the temple, should have said that the plot against Jesus was the cause that these things happened to the people, since they killed the prophesied Christ; but being not far from the truth, even unintentionally as it were, he says that these things happened to the Jews as punishment for James the Just, who was a brother of Jesus who was called the Christ, since they killed him who was altogether just.

SLAVONIC ADDITION TO THE JEWISH WAR[1]

5

"The Ministry, Trial and Crucifixion of 'The Wonder-Worker' [Jesus]."[2]

a   "At that time there appeared a man, if it is permissable to call him a man. His nature [and form] were human, but his appearance [was something] more than [that] of a man; [notwithstanding his works were divine]. He worked miracles wonderful and mighty. [Therefore it is impossible for me to call him a man]; but again, if I look at the nature which he shared with all, I will not call him an angel. And everything whatsoever he wrought through an invisible power, he wrought by word and command. Some said of him, 'Our first lawgiver is risen from the dead and hath performed many healings and arts,' while others thought that he was sent from God. Howbeit in many things he disobeyed the Law and kept not the Sabbath according to [our]
b   fathers' customs. Yet, on the other hand, he did nothing shameful; nor [did he do anything] with aid of hands, but by word alone did he provide everything. And many of the multitude followed after him and hearkened to his teaching; and many souls were in commotion, thinking that thereby the Jewish tribes might free themselves from Roman hands. Now it was his custom in general to sojourn over against the city upon the Mount of Olives; and there, too, he bestowed his healings upon the people.

"And there assembled unto him of ministers one hundred and fifty, and a multitude of the people. Now when they saw his power, that he accomplished whatsoever he would by [a] word, and when they had made known to him their will, that he should enter into the city and cut down the Roman troops and Pilate, and rule over us, he disdained us not.[3]

"And when thereafter knowledge of it came to the Jewish leaders, they assembled together with the high-priest and spake:
c   'We are powerless and [too] weak to withstand the Romans. Seeing, moreover, that the bow is bent, we will go and communicate to Pilate what we have heard, and shall be clear of

---

Josephus, Slavonic Addition to the *Jewish War*, II. 9. 3, with permission of the Harvard University Press.
[1]The interpolation in the account of the administration of Pilate as translated by H. St. J. Thackeray from the edition of Berendts and Grass.
[2]Supposed interpolations, according to Eisler's critical edition of the text, are placed in square brackets.
[3]One MS has: "but he heeded not."

Tacitus

6

Ergo abolendo rumori Nero subdidit reos et quaesitissimis poenis adfecit, quos per flagitia inuisos uulgus Christianos appellabat. auctor nominis eius Christus Tiberio imperitante per procuratorem Pontium Pilatum supplicio adfectus erat; repressaque in praesens exitiabilis superstitio rursum erumpebat, non modo per Iudaeam, originem eius mali, sed per urbem etiam, quo cuncta undique atrocia aut pudenda confluunt celebranturque. igitur primum correpti qui fatebantur, deinde indicio eorum multitudo ingens haud proinde in crimine incendii quam odio humani generis conuicti sunt.

Tacitus *Ann.* XV.44.2, cf. Clemens *Ad Corinthios* VI.

trouble, lest he hear [it] from others, and we be robbed of our substance and ourselves slaughtered and our children scattered.' And they went and communicated [it] to Pilate. And he sent and had many of the multitude slain. And he had the Wonder-worker brought up, and after instituting an inquiry concerning him, he pronounced judgment: 'He is [a benefactor, not] a malefactor, [nor] a rebel, [nor] covetous of kingship.' [And he let him go; for he had healed his dying wife.]

" [And he went to his wonted place and did his wonted works. And when more people again assembled round him, he glorified himself through his actions more than all. The teachers of the Law were overcome with envy, and gave thirty talents to Pilate, in order that he should put him to death. And he took [it] and gave them liberty to execute their will themselves.] And they laid hands on him and crucified him contrary to the law of [their] fathers."[1]

[1] The Rumanian Josephus reads: " according to the law of the emperors."
A. Berendts, *Die Zeugnisse vom Christentum im slavischen "De bello Judaico" des Josephus* (T. u. U., Neue Folge, XIV. Band, Heft 4), 1906; H. St. John Thackeray, *Selections from Josephus*, London, 1919; ———, *Josephus the Man and the Historian* (The Hilda Stroock Lectures), New York, 1929; R. Eisler, *The Messiah Jesus and John the Baptist according to Flavius Josephus' recently rediscovered "Capture of Jerusalem" and the other Jewish and Christian Sources*, English ed. by A. H. Krappe, New York, 1931.

B. Gentile Sources

TACITUS (c. A. D. 55-117)

6

Therefore, in order to disprove the rumor[1], Nero falsely accused culprits and subjected to most unusual punishments those whom, hated for their shameful deeds, the populace called Christians. The author of this name, Christ, was put to " death " by the procurator, Pontius Pilate, while Tiberius was emperor; but the dangerous superstition, though suppressed for the moment, broke out again not only in Judea, the origin of this evil, but even in the city, where all atrocious and shameful things flow together from all sides and are practised. First, therefore,

[1] I.e. that he, Nero, had ordered the fire—which occurred in the summer of A.D. 64.

Suetonius

7

Iudaeos impulsore Chresto assidue tumultuantes Roma expulit.

Suetonius *Claud.* XXV, cf. Dio LX.6; Orosius VII.6; Acta Ap. 18.2.

8

Afflicti suppliciis Christiani, genus hominum superstitionis nouae ac maleficae.

Suetonius *Nero* XVI, cf. Plinius *Epist.* X.96,97; Tertullianus *Apol.* II et V; Lucianus *De morte Perigrini* XI.

C. Plinius Traiano Imperatori

9

Solemne est mihi, domine, omnia, de quibus dubito, ad te referre. quis enim potest melius uel cunctationem meam regere, uel ignorantiam instruere? cognitionibus de Christianis interfui numquam: ideo nescio quid et quatenus aut puniri soleat, aut quaeri. nec mediocriter haesitaui, sitne aliquod discrimen aetatun, an quamlibet teneri nihil a robustioribus differant, detur paenitentiae uenia, an ei, qui omnino Christianus fuit, desisse non prosit, nomen ipsum, etiamsi flagitiis careat, an flagitia cohaerentia nomini puniantur.

those were seized who confessed [that they were Christians]; then, upon their information, a great multitude was convicted not so much upon the charge of setting fire [to the city] as for hatred of the human race.

C. H. Dodd, *History and the Gospel* (New York, 1938), pp. 106f.; F. R. Montgomery Hitchcock, " The Charge against the Christians in Tacitus," *Church Quarterly Review*, Vol. 109, 218 (1930), pp. 300–316; H. Fuchs, " Tacitus über die Christen," *Vigiliae Christianae*, Vol. IV, 2 (1950), pp. 65–93.

SUETONIUS (c. A. D. 75–160)

7

He (Claudius) expelled from Rome the Jews who were constantly stirring up a tumult under the leadership of Chrestus.

H. Jannes, " Impulsore Chresto," *Annuari de l' Institut Philol. et d' Hist. Orientalis*, (Méllanges Bidez, Vol. 2, 1934), pp. 531–553.

8

The Christians were put to death, a " sect " of men of a recent and wicked superstition.

PLINY TO TRAJAN (A. D. 111)

9

a " It is a rule, Noble Sir, which I inviolably observe, to refer myself to you in all my doubts; for who is more capable of guiding my uncertainty or informing my ignorance? Having never been present at any trials of the Christians, I am unacquainted with the method and limits to be observed either in examining or punishing them. Whether any difference is to be made on account of age, or no distinction allowed between the youngest and the adults; whether repentance admits to a pardon, or if a man has been once a Christian it avails him nothing to recant; whether the mere profession of Christianity, albeit without crimes, or only the crimes associated therewith are punishable—in all these points I am greatly doubtful.

Interim in iis, qui ad me tamquam Christiani deferebantur, hunc sum secutus modum. interrogaui ipsos, an essent Christiani. confitentes iterum ac tertio interrogaui, supplicium minatus. perseuerantes duci iussi. neque enim dubitabam, qualecunque esset, quod faterentur, pertinaciam certe et inflexibilem obstinationem debere puniri. fuerunt alii similis amentiae quos, quia ciues Romani erant, adnotaui in urbem remittendos.

Mox ipso tractatu, ut fieri solet, diffundente se crimine plures species inciderunt. propositus est libellus sine auctore multorum nomina continens. qui negabant se esse Christianos aut fuisse, cum praeeunte me deos appellarent, et imagini tuae, quam propter hoc iusseram cum simulacris numinum adferri, ture ac uino supplicarent, praetera maledicerent Christo, quorum nihil posse cogi dicuntur, qui sunt re uera Christiani, dimittendos esse putaui. alii ab indice nominati esse se Christianos dixerunt et mox negauerunt; fuisse quidem, sed desisse, quidam ante triennium, quidam ante plures annos, non nemo etiam ante uiginti quinque. omnes et imaginem tuam deorumque simulacra uenerati sunt: et Christo maledixerunt.

Adfirmabant autem hanc fuisse summam uel culpae suae uel erroris, quod essent soliti stato die ante lucem conuenire carmenque Christo quasi deo dicere secum inuicem seque sacramento non in scelus aliquod obstringere, sed ne furta, ne latrocinia, ne adulteria committerent, ne fidem fallerent, ne depositum appellati abnegarent. quibus peractis morem sibi discedendi fuisse rursusque coeundi ad capiendum cibum, promiscuum tamen et innoxium; quod ipsum facere desisse post edictum meum, quo secundum mandata tua hetaerias esse uetueram. quo magis necessarium credidi ex duabus ancillis, quae ministrae dicebantur, quid esset ueri et per tormenta quaerere. sed nihil aliud inueni, quam superstitionem prauam, immodicam.

"In the meanwhile, the method I have observed towards
b those who have been denounced to me as Christians is this: I
interrogated them whether they were Christians; if they confessed it I repeated the question twice again, adding the threat of
capital punishment; if they still persevered, I ordered them to be
executed. For whatever the nature of their creed might be, I
could at least feel no doubt that contumacy and inflexible
obstinacy deserved chastisement. There were others also
possessed with the same infatuation, but being citizens of Rome,
I directed them to be carried thither.

"These accusations spread, as is usually the case, from the
mere fact of the matter being investigated and several forms of
the mischief came to light. A placard was put up, without any
signature, accusing a large number of persons by name. Those
who denied they were, or had ever been, Christians, who
repeated after me an invocation to the Gods, and offered adoration, with wine and frankincense, to your image, which I had
ordered to be brought for that purpose, together with those of
the Gods, and who finally cursed Christ—none of which acts, it
is said, those who are really Christians can be forced into per-
c forming—these I thought it proper to discharge. Others who
were named by that informer at first confessed themselves
Christians, and then denied it; true, they had been of that
persuasion but they had quitted it, some three years, some many
years, and a few as much as twenty-five years ago. They all
worshipped your statue and the images of the Gods, and cursed
Christ.

"They affirmed, however, the whole of their guilt, or their
error, was that they were in the habit of meeting on a certain
fixed day before it was light, when they sang in alternate verses a
hymn to Christ, as to a god, and bound themselves by a solemn
oath, not to any wicked deeds, but never to commit any fraud,
theft or adultery, never to falsify their word, nor deny a trust
when they should be called upon to deliver it up; after which it
was their custom to separate, and then reassemble to partake of
food—but food of an ordinary and innocent kind. Even this
practice, however, they had abandoned after the publication
of my edict, by which, according to your orders, I had forbidden
d political associations. I judge it so much the more necessary to
extract the real truth, with the assistance of torture, from two
female slaves, who were styled deaconesses: but I could discover
nothing more than depraved and excessive superstition.

"I, therefore, adjourned the proceedings, and betook myself

Ideo dilata cognitione ad consulendum te decurri. uisa est enim mihi res digna consultatione, maxime propter periclitantium numerum. multi enim omnis aetatis, omnis ordinis, utriusque sexus etiam, uocantur in periculum et uocabuntur. neque enim ciuitates tantum, sed uicos etiam atque agros superstitionis istius contagio peruagata est; quae uidetur sisti et corrigi posse. certe satis constat, prope iam desolata templa coepisse celebrari, et sacra solemnia diu intermissa repeti: passimque uenire uictimas, quarum adhuc rarissimus emptor inueniebatur. ex quo facile est opinari, quae turba hominum emendari possit, si fiat paenitentiae locus.

Traianus Plinio

Actum quem debuisti, mi Secunde, in excutiendis causis eorum, qui Christiani ad te delati fuerant, secutus es. neque enim in uniuersum aliquid, quod quasi certam formam habeat, constitui potest. conquirendi non sunt; si deferantur et arguantur, puniendi sunt, ita tamen, ut, qui negauerit se Christianum esse idque re ipsa manifestum fecerit, id est supplicando diis nostris, quamuis suspectus in praeteritum fuerit, ueniam ex paenitentia impetret. sine auctore uero propositi libelli nullo crimine locum habere debent. nam et pessimi exempli, nec nostri saeculi est.

Plinius *Epistolae* X. xcvi–xcvii.

at once to your counsel. For the matter seemed to me well worth referring to you,—especially considering the numbers endangered. Persons of all ranks and ages, and of both sexes are, and will be, involved in the prosecution. For this contagious superstition is not confined to the cities only, but has spread through the villages and rural districts; it seems possible, however, to check and cure it. 'Tis certain at least that the temples, which had been almost deserted, begin now to be frequented; and the sacred festivals, after a long intermission, are again revived; while there is a general demand for sacrificial animals, which for some time past have met with but few purchasers. From hence it is easy to imagine what multitude may be reclaimed from this error, if a door be left open to repentance.

TRAJAN TO PLINY

e " The method you have pursued, my dear Pliny, in sifting the cases of those denounced to you as Christians is extremely proper. It is not possible to lay down any general rule which can be applied as the fixed standard in all cases of this nature. No search should be made for these people; when they are denounced and found guilty they must be punished; with the restriction, however, that when the party denies himself to be a Christian, and shall give proof that he is not, that is by adoring our Gods, he shall be pardoned on the ground of repentance, even though he may have formerly incurred suspicion. Informations without the accuser's name subscribed must not be admitted in evidence against anyone, as it is introducing a very dangerous precedent, and by no means agreeable to the spirit of the age."

Translation by William Melmoth and revised by W. M. L. Hutchinson, *Letters of Pliny*, Vol. II (*Loeb Classical Library*), pp. 400ff., by the courtesy of the Harvard University Press.
A. I. Kleffner, *Der Briefwechsel zwischen dem jüngern Plinius und Kaiser Trajan die Christen betreffend. Wert und Bedeutung desselben für die älteste Kirchengeschichte*, Paderborn, 1907; Helen H. Tanzer, *The Letters of Pliny the Younger, Selected and Edited together with a Companion to Pliny's Letters*, New York, 1936; Robert M. Grant, " Pliny and the Christians," *Harvard Theological Review*, Vol. 41 (1948), pp. 273-274.

Hadrianus Minucio Fundano

10

Accepi litteras ad me scriptas a decessore tuo Serennio Graniano clarissimo uiro et non placet mihi relationem silentio praeterire, ne et innoxii perturbentur et calumniatoribus latrocinandi tribuatur occasio. itaque si euidenter prouinciales huic petitioni suae adesse ualent aduersum Christianos, ut pro tribunali eos in aliquo arguant, hoc eis exequi non prohibeo. precibus autem in hoc solis et adclamationibus uti eis non permitto. etenim multo aequius est, si quis uolet accusare, te cognoscere de obiectis. si quis igitur accusat et probat aduersum leges quicquam agere memoratos homines, pro merito peccatorum etiam supplicia statues. illud mehercule magnopere curabis, ut si quis calumniae gratia quemquam horum postulauerit reum, in hunc pro sui nequitia suppliciis seuerioribus uindices.

Iustinus *Apologia* 68.6.

Epictetus

11

Ἄν τις . . . οὕτως δὲ καὶ οὗτος τὰς μὲν ὕλας παρ' οὐδὲν ᾖ πεποιημένας, τὴν παιδίαν δὲ τὴν περὶ αὐτὰς καὶ ἀναστροφὴν ἀσπάζηται· ποῖος ἔτι τούτῳ τύραννος φοβερὸς ἢ ποῖοι δορυφόροι ἢ ποῖαι μάχαιραι αὐτῶν;

Εἶτα ὑπὸ μανίας μὲν δύναταί τις οὕτως διατεθῆναι πρὸς ταῦτα καὶ ὑπὸ ἔθους οἱ Γαλιλαῖοι· ὑπὸ λόγου δὲ καὶ ἀποδείξεως οὐδεὶς δύναται μαθεῖν, ὅτι ὁ θεὸς πάντα πεποίηκεν τὰ ἐν τῷ κόσμῳ καὶ αὐτὸν τὸν κόσμον ὅλον μὲν ἀκώλυτον καὶ αὐτοτελῆ, τὰ ἐν μέρει δ' αὐτοῦ πρὸς χρείαν τῶν ὅλων; . . .

Epictetus *Dissertationes* IV.7.5–6.

Gentile Sources

HADRIAN'S RESCRIPT TO MINUCIUS FUNDANUS[1]

10

I have received a letter written to me from your predecessor, his most excellent Serennius Granianus, and I think that the correspondence ought not to pass by in silence, lest innocent people would be harassed as well as occasion of villany be allowed the false accusers. Therefore, if the people, in the provinces can sustain this petition of theirs against the Christians concretely so as to accuse them in court in any respect, I do not prohibit them to go through with this, but I do not allow them to make use of mere entreaties and slogans. For it is by far fairer, if anyone wishes to accuse, that you investigate about the accusations. If, therefore, someone accuses and proves that the said persons are doing anything against the laws, you will determine the penalties according to the "nature" of the offences; but, by Hercules, be extremely careful, if anyone have accused someone of these [Christians] as guilty with a false accusation, that you inflict severer penalties upon him for his wickedness.

[1] Governor of Asia c. A. D. 125.

EPICTETUS (c. A. D. 50-120)

11

"If a man . . . has reckoned the material things of life as nothing, but is glad to play with them and handle them—what kind of tyrant, or guards, or swords in the hands of guards can any more instil fear in the breast of such a man?

"Therefore, if madness can produce this attitude of mind toward the things, which have just been mentioned, and also habit, as with the Galileans, cannot reason and demonstration teach a man that God has made all things in the universe, and the universe itself, to be free from hindrance, and to contain its end in itself, and the parts of it to serve the needs of the whole?"

[1] Published from Stenographic notes by Flavius Arrian (c. A. D. 190-220). Translated by W. A. Oldfather, *Arrian's Discourses of Epictetus*, Vol. II (*Loeb Classical Library*) pp. 361f., with permission of the Harvard University Press.

Theodore Zahn, *Der Stoiker Epiktet und sein Verhältnis zum Christentum*, Erlangen, 1895.

Lapis Tiburtinus

13

[P. SVLPICIVS P. F. QVIRINIVS COS.
....
PR. PRO CONSVL. CRETAM ET CYRENAS PROVINCIAM OPTINVIT
....
LEGATVS PR. PR. DIVI AVGVSTI SYRIAM ET PHOENICEN OPTINENS
BELLVM GESSIT CVM GENTE HOMONADEN-
SIVM QVAE INTERFECERAT AMYNTAM
R]EGEM · QVA · REDACTA · IN · POT[ESTATEM IMP. CAESARIS]

MARA,[1] THE SON OF SERAPION, TO HIS SON, SERAPION[2]

12

" For what else have we to say, when wise men are forcibly dragged by the hands of tyrants, and their wisdom is taken captive by calumny, and they are oppressed in their intelligence without defence? For what advantage did the Athenians gain by the murder of Socrates, the recompense of which they received in famine and pestilence? Or the people of Samos by the burning of Pythagoras, because in one hour their country was entirely covered with sand? Or the Jews by the death of their wise king, because from that time their kingdom was taken away? For with justice did God make recompense to the wisdom of these three: for the Athenians died of famine; and the Samians were overwhelmed by the sea without remedy; and the Jews, desolate and driven from their own kingdom, are scattered through every country. Socrates is not dead, because of Plato; neither Pythagoras, because of the statue of Juno (Hera); nor the Wise King, because of the laws which he promulgated."

[1]Probably a Syrian Stoic of the first or second century.
[2]An extract from the letter written probably between A. D. 73-160. Translated by William Cureton, *Spicilegium-Syriacum*, p. 73 (with notes).

THE INSCRIPTION OF TIBUR[1]

13

Publius Sulpicius son of Publius Quirinius[2] consul

praetor proconsul obtained the Province Crete and Cyrene

legate propraetor of the divine Augustus obtaining Syria and Phoenicia waged war with the nation of the Homonadenses which had killed Amyntas the King[3]. *Which having been restored to the power* of the Emperor, Caesar *Augustus, and of the Roman*

[1]Mommsen says: " I do not put forward a new and recondite opinion; but agreeing with the same learned men (Sanclement, Borghesi, Henzen, Nipperdey), I shall demonstrate briefly first that the inscription cannot refer to C. Sentius Saturninus; then, in respect to Quirinius, not only that nothing opposes but that the indications considered above and chiefly the double Syrian legation so converge on him that the attribution by Sanclement [to Quirinius] is to be regarded not only as probable but as clearly proven."
[2]Cf. Lk. 2 : 2.
[3] Of the Galatians; slain by the Homonadenses in 25 B. C.

AVGVSTI · POPVLIQVE · ROMANI · SENATV[S DIS IMMORTALIBVS]
SVPPLICATIONES · BINAS · OB · RES · PROSP[ERE AB EO GESTAS ET]
IPSE · ORNAMENTA · TRIVMPH[ALIA DECREVIT]
PRO · CONSVL · ASIAM · PROVINCIAM · OP[TINVIT LEGATVS PR. PR.
DIVI · AVGVSTI [I]TERVM SYRIAM · ET · PH[OENICEN OPTINVIT]

Cf. Th. Mommsen, *Res gestae diui Augusti* (Berlin, 1883), p. 177; C. I. L., XIV.3613.

14

Τιβέρ[ιος Κλαύδιος Κ]αῖσ[αρ Σεβαστ]ὸς Γ[ερμανικός, ἀρχιερεὺς μέγιστος, δημαρχικῆς ἐξου-]
σίας [τὸ ιβ', αὐτοκράτωρ τ]ὸ κϛ', π[ατὴρ π]ατρί[δος, ὕπατος τὸ ε', τιμητής, Δελφῶν τῆι πόλει χαίρειν].
Πάλ[αι μὲν]· τῆι π[όλει τ]ῶν Δελφ[ῶν πρόθ]υμο[ς ἐγενόμην . . . . καὶ εὔνους ἐξ ἀρ-]
χῆς, ἀεὶ [δ'] ἐτήρη[σα τὴ]ν θρησκεί[αν τ]οῦ Ἀπό[λλωνος τοῦ Πυθίου . . . . ὅσα δὲ]
νῦν λέγεται καὶ [πολ]ειτῶν ἔρι[δες ἐ]κεῖναι ω . . . . [καθὼς Λούκιος Ἰού-]
νιος Γαλλίων ὁ φ[ίλος] μου κα[ὶ ἀνθύ]πατος [τῆς Ἀχαΐας ἔγραψεν . . . . διὰ τοῦτο συγχωρῶ ὑμᾶς]
ἔτι ἕξειν τὸν πρό[τερ]ο[ν . . . .] || ε[. . . . τῶν ἄλ-]

Adolf Deissmann, "*Paul, A Study in Social and Religious History*," translated by W. E. Wilson (London, 1926), p. 272.

Epistola Abgari ad Iesum

15

Ἄβγαρος Οὐχαμα τοπάρχης Ἰησοῦ σωτῆρι ἀγαθῷ ἀναφανέντι ἐν τόπῳ Ἱεροσολύμων χαίρειν. ἤκουσταί μοι τὰ περὶ σοῦ καὶ τῶν σῶν ἰαμάτων, ὡς ἄνευ φαρμάκων καὶ βοτανῶν ὑπὸ σοῦ γινομένων. ὡς γὰρ λόγος, τυφλοὺς ἀναβλέπειν ποιεῖς, χωλοὺς περιπατεῖν, καὶ λεπροὺς καθαρίζεις, καὶ ἀκάθαρτα πνεύματα καὶ δαίμονας ἐκβάλλεις, καὶ τοὺς ἐν μακρονοσίᾳ βασανιζομένους θεραπεύεις, καὶ νεκροὺς ἐγείρεις. καὶ ταῦτα πάντα ἀκούσας περὶ σοῦ, κατὰ νοῦν

People, the Senate decreed to the immortal gods *double supplications because of affairs prosperous*ly *completed* by him and *to him triumphal insignia* . . . *proconsul* obtained *the Province Asia*, legate propraetor *of the divine Augustus* obtained *again Syria and* Phoenicia.

> W. M. Ramsay, *The Bearing of Recent Discovery on the Trustworthiness of the New Testament* (Reprinted, Grand Rapids, 1953), pp. 238-300; W. Lodder, *Die Schätzung des Quirinius bei Flavius Josephus*, Leipzig, 1930; Walter Bauer, *Griechisch-Deutsches Wörterbuch zu den Schriften des Neuen Testaments und der übrigen urchristlichen Literatur*, 4. völlig neu bearbeitete Auflage, Berlin (1952), *s. v.* Quirinius.

GALLIO INSCRIPTION (*c.* A. D. 51-53)

14

*Ti*berius Claudius *C*aesar Augus*tus* Germanicus, Chief Highpriest[1] . . . for the 12th time invested with tribunician pow*er*, for 26 times Imperator, Father of the F*atherl*and, Consul for the 5th time, Censor, greetings to the city of the Delphians.

Since long ago I have been zealous *for the city of the Delph*ians . . . and from the begin*ning* [have I been] well-disposed, and I *have always observed* the *worsh*ip of *the* Pythian *Apoll*o . . . , but as much *as is now said and those strife*s *of* the citi*z*ens . . . as Lucius J*un*i*us* Gallio, *my f*riend, *and* Proconsul of Achaea wrote . . . for this reason I allow you to have *even yet the former* . . . .

[1] I.e. Pontifex Maximus.
Adolf Deissmann, *op. cit.*, pp. 269-284, for a brief discussion and literature.

C. Christian Sources

LETTER OF ABGAR TO JESUS (*c.* A. D. 250)

15

Abgar Uchama, the Toparch, to Jesus, the Good Saviour who has appeared in the region of Jerusalem, greeting.

I have heard matters concerning you and the healings which are brought about by you without medicine and herbs. For according to the report you are making the blind to see, the lame to walk, you are cleansing lepers, you are casting out unclean spirits and demons, you are healing those long afflicted, and you are raising the dead. Since I have heard all these things about you,

ἐθέμην τὸ ἕτερον τῶν δύο, ἢ ὅτι σὺ εἶ ὁ θεὸς καὶ καταβὰς ἀπὸ τοῦ οὐρανοῦ ποιεῖς ταῦτα, ἢ υἱὸς εἶ τοῦ θεοῦ ποιῶν ταῦτα. διὰ τοῦτο τοίνυν γράψας ἐδεήθην σου σκυλῆναι πρός με καὶ τὸ πάθος, ὃ ἔχω, θεραπεῦσαι. καὶ γὰρ ἤκουσα ὅτι καὶ Ἰουδαῖοι καταγογγύζουσί σου καὶ βούλονται κακῶσαί σε. πόλις δὲ μικροτάτη μοί ἐστι καὶ σεμνή, ἥτις ἐξαρκεῖ ἀμφοτέροις.

Rescriptum Iesu ad Abgarum

Μακάριος εἶ πιστεύσας ἐν ἐμοί, μὴ ἑορακώς με. γέγραπται γὰρ περὶ ἐμοῦ τοὺς ἑορακότας με μὴ πιστεύσειν ἐν ἐμοί, καὶ ἵνα οἱ μὴ ἑορακότες με αὐτοὶ πιστεύσωσι καὶ ζήσονται. περὶ δὲ οὗ ἔγραψάς μοι ἐλθεῖν πρὸς σέ, δέον ἐστὶ πάντα δι' ἃ ἀπεστάλην ἐνταῦθα, πληρῶσαι καὶ μετὰ τὸ πληρῶσαι οὕτως ἀναληφθῆναι πρὸς τὸν ἀποστείλαντά με. καὶ ἐπειδὰν ἀναληφθῶ, ἀποστελῶ σοί τινα τῶν μαθητῶν μου, ἵνα ἰάσηταί σου τὸ πάθος καὶ ζωήν σοι καὶ τοῖς σὺν σοὶ παράσχηται.

Eusebius H.E. I.13.6–10.

Irenaeus

16

Καὶ πάντες οἱ πρεσβύτεροι μαρτυροῦσιν οἱ κατὰ τὴν Ἀσίαν Ἰωάννῃ τῷ τοῦ κυρίου μαθητῇ συμβεβληκότες παραδεδωκέναι τὸν Ἰωάννην. παρέμεινεν γὰρ αὐτοῖς μέχρι τῶν Τραϊανοῦ χρόνων . . . . ἀλλὰ καὶ ἡ ἐν Ἐφέσῳ ἐκκλησία ὑπὸ Παύλου μὲν τεθεμελιωμένη, Ἰωάννου δὲ παραμείναντος αὐτοῖς μέχρι τῶν Τραϊανοῦ χρόνων, μάρτυς ἀληθής ἐστιν τῆς τῶν ἀποστόλων παραδόσεως.

Irenaeus C. haer. II.22.5, cf. Eusebius H.E. III.23.3 et 6; Clemens Alexandrinus De diuite seruando 42; Tertullianus De praescr. haer. 36.

Irenaeus Florino

17

Ταῦτα τὰ δόγματα, Φλωρῖνε, ἵνα πεφεισμένως εἴπω, οὐκ ἔστιν ὑγιοῦς γνώμης· ταῦτα τὰ δόγματα ἀσύμφωνά ἐστι τῇ ἐκκλησίᾳ εἰς τὴν μεγίστην ἀσέβειαν περιβάλλοντα τοὺς πειθομένους αὐτοῖς· ταῦτα τὰ δόγματα οὐδὲ οἱ ἔξω τῆς ἐκκλησίας αἱρετικοὶ ἐτόλμησαν

I decided either that you are God come down from heaven [to] do these things or that you are a son of God, since you are doing these things. Therefore, then, I write asking you to take the trouble to come and heal the affliction which I have. For I have heard also that even the Jews are murmuring against you and are planning to do you harm. Now I have a very small but venerable city which is sufficient for both of us.

Reply of Jesus to Abgar

Blessed are you for believing in me, although you have not seen me. For it is written concerning me that those who have seen me will not believe in me, and that those who have not seen me they will believe and be saved. But concerning what you wrote to me, namely to come to you, it is necessary [for me] to complete here all for which I was sent and after the completion to be received up to Him that sent me. But when I am received up, I shall send one of my disciples to you to heal your affliction and to impart life to you and your people.

Ernst von Dobschütz, *Christusbilder. Untersuchungen zur christlichen Legende*, (*T. u. U.*, Neue Folge, 3. Band), 1899; H. J. Lawlor and J. E. L. Oulton, *Eusebius, The Ecclesiastical History and the Martyrs of Palestine*, Vol. II (London, 1928), p. 57.

IRENAEUS (c. A. D. 125/140–200)

16

And all the presbyters, who associated in Asia with John, the disciple of the Lord, testify that John handed down [these things]. For he remained with them until the times of Trajan.[1] ... And also the church in Ephesus founded by Paul—John having remained with them until the times of Trajan—is a true[2] witness of the tradition of the Apostles.

[1] A. D. 98–117. [2] I.e. faithful.

IRENAEUS TO FLORINUS

17

a These doctrines, Florinus,[1] I speak mildly, are not of sound opinion. These doctrines are not in accord with the Church [and] lead those who are persuaded by them into very great impiety. These doctrines not even the heretics outside the

[1] A Roman presbyter who became a Valentinian about A. D. 190.

ἀποφήνασθαί ποτε. ταῦτα τὰ δόγματα οἱ πρὸ ἡμῶν πρεσβύτεροι, οἱ καὶ τοῖς ἀποστόλοις συμφοιτήσαντες, οὐ παρέδωκάν σοι. εἶδον γάρ σε, παῖς ἔτι ὤν, ἐν τῇ κάτω Ἀσίᾳ παρὰ Πολυκάρπῳ λαμπρῶς πράσσοντα ἐν τῇ βασιλικῇ αὐλῇ καὶ πειρώμενον εὐδοκομεῖν παρ' αὐτῷ. μᾶλλον γὰρ τὰ τότε διαμνημονεύω τῶν ἐναγχος γινομένων (αἱ γὰρ ἐκ παιδῶν μαθήσεις συναύξουσαι τῇ ψυχῇ, ἑνοῦνται αὐτῇ), ὥστε με δύνασθαι εἰπεῖν καὶ τὸν τόπον ἐν ᾧ καθεζόμενος διελέγετο ὁ μακάριος Πολύκαρπος, καὶ τὰς προόδους αὐτοῦ καὶ τὰς εἰσόδους καὶ τὸν χαρακτῆρα τοῦ βίου καὶ τὴν τοῦ σώματος ἰδέαν καὶ τὰς διαλέξεις ἃς ἐποιεῖτο πρὸς τὸ πλῆθος, καὶ τὴν μετὰ Ἰωάννου συναναστροφὴν ὡς ἀπήγγελλεν καὶ τὴν μετὰ τῶν λοιπῶν τῶν ἑορακότων τὸν κύριον, καὶ ὡς ἀπεμνημόνευεν τοὺς λόγους αὐτῶν, καὶ περὶ τοῦ κυρίου τίνα ἦν ἃ παρ' ἐκείνων ἀκηκόει, καὶ περὶ τῶν δυνάμεων αὐτοῦ, καὶ περὶ τῆς διδασκαλίας, ὡς παρὰ τῶν αὐτοπτῶν τῆς ζωῆς τοῦ λόγου παρειληφὼς ὁ Πολύκαρπος ἀπήγγελλεν πάντα σύμφωνα ταῖς γραφαῖς. ταῦτα καὶ τότε διὰ τὸ ἔλεος τοῦ θεοῦ τὸ ἐπ' ἐμοὶ γεγονὸς σπουδαίως ἤκουον, ὑπομνηματιζόμενος αὐτὰ οὐκ ἐν χάρτῃ, ἀλλ' ἐν τῇ ἐμῇ καρδίᾳ· καὶ ἀεὶ διὰ τὴν χάριν τοῦ θεοῦ γνησίως αὐτὰ ἀναμαρυκῶμαι, καὶ δύναμαι διαμαρτύρασθαι ἔμπροσθεν τοῦ θεοῦ ὅτι εἴ τι τοιοῦτον ἀκηκόει ἐκεῖνος ὁ μακάριος καὶ ἀποστολικὸς πρεσβύτερος, ἀνακράξας ἂν καὶ ἐμφράξας τὰ ὦτα αὐτοῦ καὶ κατὰ τὸ σύνηθες αὐτῷ εἰπὼν *Ὦ καλὲ θεέ, εἰς οἵους με καιροὺς τετήρηκας, ἵνα τούτων ἀνέχωμαι, πεφεύγει ἂν καὶ τὸν τόπον ἐν ᾧ καθεζόμενος ἢ ἑστὼς τῶν τοιούτων ἀκηκόει λόγων. καὶ ἐκ τῶν ἐπιστολῶν δὲ αὐτοῦ ὧν ἐπέστειλεν ἤτοι ταῖς γειτνιώσαις ἐκκλησίαις, ἐπιστηρίζων αὐτάς, ἢ τῶν ἀδελφῶν τισί, νουθετῶν αὐτοὺς καὶ προτρεπόμενος, δύναται φανερωθῆναι.

Irenaeus, cf. Eusebius, H.E. V.20.4—8.

Papias

18

Τοῦ δὲ Παπία συγγράμματα πέντε τὸν ἀριθμὸν φέρεται, ἃ καὶ ἐπιγέγραπται Λογίων κυριακῶν ἐξηγήσεως. τούτων καὶ Εἰρηναῖος ὡς μόνων αὐτῷ γραφέντων μνημονεύει, ὧδέ πως λέγων·

Ταῦτα δὲ καὶ Παπίας ὁ Ἰωάννου μὲν ἀκουστής, Πολυκάρπου δὲ ἑταῖρος γεγονώς, ἀρχαῖος ἀνήρ, ἐγγράφως ἐπιμαρτυρεῖ ἐν τῇ τετάρτῃ τῶν ἑαυτοῦ βιβλίων. ἔστιν γὰρ αὐτῷ πέντε βιβλία συντεταγμένα.

Church ever dared to proclaim. These doctrines the presbyters before us, who had company even with the Apostles, did not hand down to you. For I saw you, when I was still a boy, in lower Asia with Polycarp doing brilliantly in the royal hall and attempting to win favour with him. For I remember the things of that time better than the things which have happened recently—for the experiences of youth, growing with the soul, are united with it—so that I could tell the very place in which the blessed Polycarp sat [and] taught, and his going out and coming in, and his way of life, and the form of his profile, and the addresses which

b he made to the people, and how he spoke of his association with John and the others who had seen the Lord, and how he remembered their words, and what the things were concerning the Lord, which he had heard from them, both concerning His miracles and concerning His teaching—how, having received them from eyewitnesses of the life of the Word, Polycarp reported all things in agreement with the Scriptures. Even then, through the mercy of God granted to me, I heard these things eagerly, storing them up, not on parchment, but in my heart; and ever, by the grace of God, I shall sincerely meditate[2] upon them. And I am able to witness before God that, if that blessed, apostolic presbyter had heard such as this, crying out and stopping his ears and, according to his custom [he would have] said: " O good God, for what times hast thou kept me that I should endure these things;" he would have fled from the place in which, sitting or standing, he had heard such words. And [this] can be shown from his epistles which he sent to the neighbouring churches, strengthening them, or to certain of the brethren, admonishing and exhorting them.

[2] Literally " chew."

PAPIAS (*c*. A. D. 130-140)

18

But of Papias five books are extant which are also entitled *Exposition of the Oracles of the Lord*. These Irenaeus also mentions

a as the only ones written by him, speaking more or less as follows: "And to these things Papias also, who was a hearer of John and a companion of Polycarp, a man of old,[1] testifies in writing in the fourth of his books; for he has five books in a collection."

[1] Or " an old man," referring to the time of his life when he wrote, or when he became an associate of Polycarp.

Καὶ ὁ μὲν Εἰρηναῖος ταῦτα· αὐτός γε μὴν ὁ Παπίας κατὰ τὸ προοίμιον τῶν αὐτοῦ λόγων ἀκροατὴν μὲν καὶ αὐτόπτην οὐδαμῶς ἑαυτὸν γενέσθαι τῶν ἱερῶν ἀποστόλων ἐμφαίνει, παρειληφέναι δὲ τὰ τῆς πίστεως παρὰ τῶν ἐκείνοις γνωρίμων διδάσκει δι' ὧν φησιν λέξεων·

Οὐκ ὀκνήσω δέ σοι καὶ ὅσα ποτὲ παρὰ τῶν πρεσβυτέρων καλῶς ἔμαθον καὶ καλῶς ἐμνημόνευσα, συγκατατάξαι ταῖς ἑρμηνείαις, διαβεβαιούμενος ὑπὲρ αὐτῶν ἀλήθειαν. οὐ γὰρ τοῖς τὰ πολλὰ λέγουσιν ἔχαιρον ὥσπερ οἱ πολλοί, ἀλλὰ τοῖς τἀληθῆ διδάσκουσιν, οὐδὲ τοῖς τὰς ἀλλοτρίας ἐντολὰς μνημονεύουσιν, ἀλλὰ τοῖς τὰς παρὰ τοῦ κυρίου τῇ πίστει δεδομένας καὶ ἀπ' αὐτῆς παραγινομένας τῆς ἀληθείας· εἰ δέ που καὶ παρηκολουθηκώς τις τοῖς πρεσβυτέροις ἔλθοι, τοὺς τῶν πρεσβυτέρων ἀνέκρινον λόγους, τί Ἀνδρέας ἢ τί Πέτρος εἶπεν ἢ τί Φίλιππος ἢ τί Θωμᾶς ἢ Ἰάκωβος ἢ τί Ἰωάννης ἢ Ματθαῖος ἤ τις ἕτερος τῶν τοῦ κυρίου μαθητῶν ἅ τε Ἀριστίων καὶ ὁ πρεσβύτερος Ἰωάννης, τοῦ κυρίου μαθηται, λέγουσιν. οὐ γὰρ τὰ ἐκ τῶν βιβλίων τοσοῦτόν με ὠφελεῖν ὑπελάμβανον ὅσον τὰ παρὰ ζώσης φωνῆς καὶ μενούσης.

Ἔνθα καὶ ἐπιστῆσαι ἄξιον δὶς καταριθμοῦντι αὐτῷ τὸ Ἰωάννου ὄνομα, ὧν τὸν μὲν πρότερον Πέτρῳ καὶ Ἰακώβῳ καὶ Ματθαίῳ καὶ τοῖς λοιποῖς ἀποστόλοις συγκαταλέγει, σαφῶς δηλῶν τὸν εὐαγγελιστήν, τὸν δ' ἕτερον Ἰωάννην, διαστείλας τὸν λόγον, ἑτέροις παρὰ τὸν τῶν ἀποστόλων ἀριθμὸν κατατάσσει, προτάξας αὐτοῦ τὸν Ἀριστίωνα, σαφῶς τε αὐτὸν πρεσβύτερον ὀνομάζει· ὡς καὶ διὰ τούτων ἀποδείκνυσθαι τὴν ἱστορίαν ἀληθῆ τῶν δύο κατὰ τὴν Ἀσίαν ὁμωνυμίᾳ κεχρῆσθαι εἰρηκότων δύο τε ἐν Ἐφέσῳ γενέσθαι μνήματα καὶ ἑκάτερον Ἰωάννου ἔτι νῦν λέγεσθαι· οἷς καὶ ἀναγκαῖον προσέχειν τὸν νοῦν, εἰκὸς γὰρ τὸν δεύτερον, εἰ μή τις ἐθέλοι τὸν πρῶτον, τὴν ἐπ' ὀνόματος φερομένην Ἰωάννου ἀποκάλυψιν ἑορακέναι. καὶ ὁ νῦν δὲ ἡμῖν δηλούμενος Παπίας τοὺς μὲν τῶν ἀποστόλων λόγους παρὰ τῶν αὐτοῖς παρηκολουθηκότων ὁμολογεῖ παρειληφέναι, Ἀριστίωνος δὲ καὶ τοῦ πρεσβυτέρου Ἰωάννου αὐτήκοον ἑαυτόν φησι γενέσθαι· ὀνομαστὶ γοῦν πολλάκις αὐτῶν μνημονεύσας ἐν τοῖς αὐτοῦ συγγράμμασιν τίθησιν αὐτῶν παραδόσεις.

Eusebius H.E. III.39.1–7.

And Irenaeus [says] these things. Papias himself, however, according to the preface of his books, shows that he himself was in no wise a hearer and eyewitness of the holy Apostles, but, by the words which he uses, he maintains that he had received the things of the faith from their pupils:

"But I shall not hesitate to put down for you with my interpretations also whatsoever things I well learned at one time from the presbyters and well remembered, confidently asserting
b truthfulness for them. For I did not take pleasure, as the multitude [does], in those who say many things, but in those who teach the things that are true; nor [did I take pleasure] in those who recall strange commands, but in those [who recall] the commands given by the Lord to the faith and coming from the truth itself. But, if perchance there came also anyone who had followed the presbyters, I made inquiry concerning the words of the presbyters: what Andrew or what Peter had said, or what Philip or what Thomas or James, or what John or Matthew or any other of the disciples of the Lord [had said], and what things Aristion and the presbyter John, disciples of the Lord, used to say. For I did not suppose that the things from the books would aid me so much as the things from the living and continuing voice."

Here it is worth while to notice also that he enumerates the
c name John twice, the former of these he classes with Peter and James and Matthew and the other Apostles, plainly meaning the Evangelist; but the other John, "repeating" the word, he places with others outside the number of the Apostles, placing Aristion before him; and he plainly calls him a presbyter. So that also by these things the story of those is shown to be true who have said that two [persons] in Asia used the same name and that there are two sepulchres in Ephesus and each one is still said to be [the sepulchre] of John. It is necessary also to give attention to these things for it is probable that the second—if one would not prefer the former—saw the Apocalypse which is extant in the name of John. And Papias, whom we are now [discussing], bears witness that he received the words of the Apostles from those who had followed them, but says that he was himself a hearer of Aristion and the presbyter John. At least he mentions them frequently by name and puts down their traditions in his writings.

Theodore Zahn, *Forschungen zur Geschichte des neutesatmentlichen Kanons*, Teil VI (Leipzig, 1906), pp. 109-175; C. de Boor, *Nueue Fragmente des Papias, Hegesippus und Pierius* (T. u. U., V. Band, Heft 2) (1888), pp. 167-184.

19

Παπίας Ἱεροπόλεως ἐπίσκοπος ἀκουστὴς τοῦ θεολόγου Ἰωάννου γενόμενος, Πολυκάρπου δὲ ἑταῖρος, πέντε λόγους κυριακῶν λογίων ἔγραψεν, ἐν οἷς ἀπαρίθμησιν ἀποστόλων ποιούμενος μετὰ Πέτρον καὶ Ἰωάννην, Φίλιππον καὶ Θωμᾶν καὶ Ματθαῖον εἰς μαθητὰς τοῦ κυρίου ἀνέγραψεν Ἀριστίωνα καὶ Ἰωάννην ἕτερον, ὃν καὶ πρεσβύτερον ἐκάλεσεν .... Παπίας ἐν τῷ δευτέρῳ λόγῳ λέγει, ὅτι Ἰωάννης ὁ θεολόγος καὶ Ἰάκωβος ὁ ἀδελφὸς αὐτοῦ ὑπὸ Ἰουδαίων ἀνῃρέθησαν.

Codex Baroccianus 142 (ed. de Boor).

20

Μετὰ δὲ Δομετιανὸν ἐβασίλευσε Νερούας ἔτος ἕν, ὃς ἀνακαλεσάμενος Ἰωάννην ἐκ τῆς νήσου ἀπέλυσεν οἰκεῖν ἐν Ἐφέσῳ. μόνος τότε περιὼν τῷ βίῳ ἐκ τῶν δώδεκα μαθητῶν καὶ συγγραψάμενος τὸ κατ' αὐτὸν εὐαγγέλιον μαρτυρίου κατηξίωται. . Παπίας γὰρ ὁ Ἱεραπόλεως ἐπίσκοπος, αὐτόπτης τούτου γενόμενος, ἐν τῷ δευτέρῳ λόγῳ τῶν κυριακῶν λογίων φάσκει, ὅτι ὑπὸ Ἰουδαίων ἀνῃρέθη· πληρώσας δηλαδὴ μετὰ τοῦ ἀδελφοῦ τὴν τοῦ Χριστοῦ περὶ αὐτῶν πρόρρησιν καὶ τὴν ἑαυτῶν ὁμολογίαν περὶ τούτου καὶ συγκατάθεσιν· εἰπὼν γὰρ ὁ κύριος πρὸς αὐτούς Δύνασθε πιεῖν τὸ ποτήριον ὃ ἐγὼ πίνω; καὶ κατανευσάντων προθύμως καὶ συνθεμένων, Τὸ ποτήριόν μου, φησίν, πίεσθε καὶ τὸ βάπτισμα ὃ ἐγὼ βαπτίζομαι βαπτισθήσεσθε. καὶ εἰκότως. ἀδύνατον γὰρ θεὸν ψεύσασθαι. οὕτω δὲ καὶ ὁ πολυμαθὴς Ὠριγένης ἐν τῇ κατὰ Ματθαῖον ἑρμηνείᾳ διαβεβαιοῦται, ὡς ὅτι μεμαρτύρηκεν Ἰωάννης, ἐκ τῶν διαδόχων τῶν ἀποστόλων ὑποσημαινάμενος τοῦτο μεμαθηκέναι. καὶ μὲν δὴ καὶ ὁ πολυΐστωρ Εὐσέβιος ἐν τῇ ἐκκλησιαστικῇ ἱστορίᾳ φησί Θωμᾶς μὲν τὴν Παρθίαν εἴληχεν, Ἰωάννης δὲ τὴν Ἀσίαν, πρὸς οὓς καὶ διατρίψας ἐτελεύτησεν ἐν Ἐφέσῳ.

Codex Coislinianus 305.

19

Papias, who was bishop of Hierapolis, a hearer of John the Theologian[1] and a companion of Polycarp, wrote five books of *Oracles of the Lord*, in which, when making an enumeration of the Apostles, he enrolled among the disciples of the Lord, together with Peter and John, Philip and Thomas and Matthew, [also] Aristion and another John, whom he called also a presbyter.... Papias in the second book says: "John the Theologian and James his brother were put to death by Jews."

[1] A title of the Apostle John which was current in the fourth century. It occurs in an eighth century MS and in the late cursive MSS in the superscription to the Apocalypse where it is translated " the Divine " in the A. V.

C. de Boor, *loc. cit.*

20

After Domitian Nerva reigned one year—who recalled John from the island and permitted [him] to dwell in Ephesus. He [was] the only one of the twelve disciples still living at that time, and when he had written his Gospel, he was counted worthy of martyrdom.[1] For Papias, the bishop of Hierapolis, since he was an eyewitness of this one, says in the second book of the *Oracles of the Lord* that he was put to death by Jews; having fulfilled evidently with his brother the prediction of Christ concerning them and their own confession and approval concerning this. For when the Lord said to them: "Are you able to drink the cup which I drink?" and when they had readily agreed and assented, he said, " My cup, you shall drink and with the baptism wherewith I am baptized you shall be baptized."[2] And rightly, for it is impossible that God should lie. So also the very learned Origen in his *Commentary on [the Gospel] according to Matthew* confirms that John suffered martyrdom, indicating that he had learned this from the successors of the Apostles. And also the very learned Eusebius says in his *Ecclesiastical History*: " Thomas received by lot Parthia, but John Asia where[3] he remained and died in Ephesus."

[1] Other MSS of the Chronicle read: " he died in peace. Concerning whom the learned Eusebius . . . ."
[2] Mk. 10 : 38b–39.
[3] Literally: " with whom, having spent the time, he died."

Polycrates

21

Καὶ γὰρ κατὰ τὴν Ἀσίαν μεγάλα στοιχεῖα κεκοίμηται· ἅτινα ἀναστήσεται τῇ ἐσχάτῃ ἡμέρᾳ τῆς παρουσίας τοῦ κυρίου, ἐν ᾗ ἔρχεται μετὰ δόξης ἐξ οὐρανοῦ καὶ ἀναζητήσει πάντας τοὺς ἁγίους, Φίλιππον τῶν δώδεκα ἀποστόλων, ὃς κεκοίμηται ἐν Ἱεραπόλει καὶ δύο θυγατέρες αὐτοῦ γεγηρακυῖαι παρθένοι καὶ ἡ ἑτέρα αὐτοῦ θυγάτηρ ἐν ἁγίῳ πνεύματι πολιτευσαμένη ἐν Ἐφέσῳ ἀναπαύεται· ἔτι δὲ καὶ Ἰωάννης, ὁ ἐπὶ τὸ στῆθος τοῦ κυρίου ἀναπεσών, ὃς ἐγενήθη ἱερεὺς τὸ πέταλον πεφορεκὼς καὶ μάρτυς καὶ διδάσκαλος, οὗτος ἐν Ἐφέσῳ κεκοίμηται.

Polycrates, cf. Eusebius H.E. III.31.3, cf. V.24.2.

Argumentum

22

Euangelium Iohannis manifestatum et datum est ecclesiis ab Iohanne adhuc in corpore constituto, sicut Papias nomine, Hierapolitanus, discipulus Iohannis carus, in exotericis, id est in extremis quinque libris retulit. descripsit uero euangelium dictante Iohanne recte. uerum Marcion hereticus, cum ab eo fuisset inprobatus eo quod contraria sentiebat, abiectus est ab Iohanne. is vero scripta uel epistulas ad eum pertulerat a fratribus, qui in Ponto fuerunt.

Vatic. Alex. no. 14 Biblio Latina saec. IX, cf. Oscar von Gebhardt, Adolf von Harnack, und Theodor Zahn, *Patrum apostolicorum opera* 5. Auflage (Leipzig, 1906), p. 77.

Origen

23

Πεπώκασι δὲ ποτήριον, καὶ τὸ βάπτισμα ἐβαπτίσθησαν οἱ τοῦ Ζεβεδαίου υἱοί, ἐπείπερ Ἡρώδης μὲν ἀπέκτεινεν Ἰάκωβον τὸν Ἰωάννου μαχαίρᾳ· ὁ δὲ Ῥωμαίων βασιλεύς, ὡς ἡ παράδοσις διδάσκει, κατεδίκασε τὸν Ἰωάννην μαρτυροῦντα διὰ τὸν τῆς ἀληθείας λόγον εἰς Πάτμον τὴν νῆσον.

Origen In Matt. XVI.6.

POLYCRATES[1] (c. A. D. 190)

21

For also in Asia great " Fathers " have fallen asleep who shall rise again on the last day " at " the appearing of the Lord, when He [will] come with glory from heaven and shall seek out all the saints—Philip, [one] of the twelve Apostles who has fallen asleep in Hierapolis and his two daughters who grew old as virgins; and his other daughter, who has lived in the Holy Spirit, rests in Ephesus; and John also, who leaned upon the breast of the Lord, who was a priest and wore the priestly mitre and [who was] a martyr and a teacher—he has fallen asleep in Ephesus.

[1]Bishop of Ephesus at the end of the second century, wrote to Victor. bishop of Rome, (A. D. 189-198).

ARGUMENT

22

The Gospel of John was published and given to the churches by John while still present in the body as [one], Papias by name, of Hierapolis, a beloved disciple of John, reported in [his] *Exoterics*, that is, the last five books. Indeed he wrote the Gospel correctly, while John dictated it. But Marcion, the heretic, when he was reproved by him because he held erroneous opinions, was rejected by John. He also brought letters and epistles to him from the brethren who were in Pontus.

Theodor Zahn, *Introduction to the New Testament*, Vol. III, pp. 196f.; A. v. Harnack, *Marcion: Das Evangelium vom fremden Gott, eine Monographie zur Geschichte der Grundlegung der katholischen Kirche*. 2. Verbesserte und vermehrte Auflage. (T. u. U., 3. Riehe, 15. Band), Leipzig, 1924.

ORIGEN

23

But the sons of Zebedee drank [the] cup and were baptized with the baptism,[1] since Herod indeed killed James the [brother] of John with [the] sword; but the King of the Romans, as tradition maintains, condemned John, bearing witness for the sake of the word of truth on Patmos, the island.

[1]Cf. no. 20 *supra*; Mk. 10 : 38b-39.

Martyrologium Syriacum

24

Τὰ ὀνόματα τῶν κυρίων ἡμῶν τῶν μαρτύρων καὶ νικητῶν καὶ αἱ ἡμέραι αὐτῶν ἐν αἷς ἔλαβον τοὺς στεφάνους. Μηνὶ Κανοῦν τῷ προτέρῳ. κς΄ καθ᾽ Ἕλληνας — Ὁ πρῶτος μάρτυρ ἐν Ἱεροσολύμοις, Στέφανος ὁ ἀπόστολος, ὁ κορυφαῖος τῶν μαρτύρων. καὶ κζ΄. — Ἰωάννης καὶ Ἰάκωβος οἱ ἀπόστολοι ἐν Ἱεροσολύμοις. καὶ κη΄ Κανοῦν τῷ προτέρῳ. — Ἐν Ῥώμῃ τῇ πόλει Παῦλος ἀπόστολος καὶ Συμεὼν Κηφᾶς ὁ κορυφαῖος τῶν ἀποστόλων τοῦ κυρίου ἡμῶν.

Ioh. Bapt. de Rossi et L. Duchesne, " Martyrologium Hieronimum," *Acta sanctorum*, 62, Novembris II. i (Brussels, 1894), p. LII.

Clemens Romanus

25

Διὰ ζῆλον καὶ ἔριν Παῦλος ὑπομονῆς βραβεῖον ἔδειξεν. ἑπτάκις δεσμὰ φορέσας, φυγαδευθείς, λιθασθείς, κήρυξ γενόμενος ἔν τε τῇ ἀνατολῇ καὶ ἐν τῇ δύσει, τὸ γενναῖον τῆς πίστεως αὐτοῦ κλέος ἔλαβεν, δικαιοσύνην διδάξας ὅλον τὸν κόσμον καὶ ἐπὶ τὸ τέρμα τῆς δύσεως ἐλθών. καὶ μαρτυρήσας ἐπὶ τῶν ἡγουμένων, οὕτως ἀπηλλάγη τοῦ κόσμου καὶ εἰς τὸν ἅγιον τόπον ἀνελήμφθη, ὑπομονῆς γενόμενος μέγιστος ὑπογραμμός.

Clemens *Ad Corinthios* V.5–7, cf. Eusebius *H.E.* II.22.1–2.

Descriptio Pauli

26

Καὶ ἐπορεύετο κατὰ τὴν βασιλικὴν ὁδὸν τὴν ἐπὶ Λύστραν, καὶ εἱστήκει ἀπεκδεχόμενος αὐτόν, καὶ τοὺς ἐρχομένους ἐθεώρει κατὰ τὴν μήνυσιν Τίτου. εἶδεν δὲ τὸν Παῦλον ἐρχόμενον, ἄνδρα μικρὸν τῷ μεγέθει, ψιλὸν τῇ κεφαλῇ, ἀγκύλον ταῖς κνήμαις, εὐεκτικόν, σύνοφρυν, μικρῶς ἐπίρρινον, χάριτος πλήρη· ποτὲ μὲν γὰρ ἐφαίνετο ὡς ἄνθρωπος, ποτὲ δὲ ἀγγέλου πρόσωπον εἶχεν.

Acta Pauli et Theclae, 3. Ed. R. A. Lipsius, *Acta Petri, Acta Pauli, Acta Petri et Pauli, Acta Pauli et Theclae, Acta Thaddaei*, I, Leipzig, 1891.

Christian Sources

SYRIAC MARTYROLOGY[1]

24

The Names of our Lords, the Martyrs and Victors and the Days on which they received their Crowns.

In the month of Canun, the Former.[2]

26: according to [the] Greeks: The first Martyr in Jerusalem, Stephen, the Apostle, the chief[3] of the Martyrs.

And 27: John and James, the Apostles, in Jerusalem.

And 28 of Canum, the Former: In Rome, the city, Paul [the] Apostle and Simon Cephas, the chief of the Apostles of our Lord.

[1]Revised in Nicomedia; not later than A. D. 411. [2]December. [3]First (?).

CLEMENT OF ROME (c. A. D. 96)

25

On account of jealousy and strife Paul was an example of the " zenith " of endurance. After he had been in bonds seven times, had been exiled, had been stoned, after he had been a preacher both in the East and the West,[1] he received the genuine renown of his faithfulness. He taught righteousness [to] the whole world, and reached the extremity of the West. And after he had borne witness before rulers, he so departed from the world and was taken up into the holy place, after he had become the greatest example of endurance.

[1]Cf. no. 96c, Canon Muratori; Rom 15 : 24, 28.

DESCRIPTION OF PAUL (c. A. D. 160)

26

And he (Onesiphorus) proceeded along the royal highway to Lystra and stood expecting him, and, according to the information of Titus, he inspected them that came. And he saw Paul coming, a man small in stature, bald-headed, crooked in legs, healthy, with eyebrows joining, nose rather long,[1] full of grace; for sometimes he appeared like a man, but sometimes he had the face of an angel.

[1]" nose somewhat hooked "—M. R. James, *The Acts of Paul*, (*The Apocryphal New Testament*, Oxford, reprinted 1926), p. 273.

Gaius

27

Γάϊος, οὗ φωνὰς ἤδη πρότερον παρατέθειμαι, ἐν τῇ φερομένῃ αὐτοῦ ζητήσει ταῦτα περὶ αὐτοῦ γράφει.

Ἀλλὰ καὶ Κήρινθος ὁ δι' ἀποκαλύψεων ὡς ὑπὸ ἀποστόλου μεγάλου γεγραμμένων τερατολογίας ἡμῖν ὡς δι' ἀγγέλων αὐτῷ δεδειγμένας ψευδόμενος ἐπεισάγει, λέγων μετὰ τὴν ἀνάστασιν ἐπίγειον εἶναι τὸ βασίλειον τοῦ χριστοῦ καὶ πάλιν ἐπιθυμίαις καὶ ἡδοναῖς ἐν Ἱερουσαλὴμ τὴν σάρκα πολιτευομένην δουλεύειν. καὶ ἐχθρὸς ὑπάρχων ταῖς γραφαῖς τοῦ θεοῦ, ἀριθμὸν χιλιονταετίας ἐν γάμῳ ἑορτῆς, θέλων πλανᾶν, λέγει γίνεσθαι.

Gaius, cf. Eusebius *H.E.* III.28.1-2.

GAIUS (BISHOP AT ROME, A. D. 283-296)

27

Gaius, whose opinions I have already stated previously, writes these things about him in his extant *Discussion*: " But Cerinthus also, by means of revelations purported to have been written by the great Apostle, lying, foists wonderful stories upon us, as if they were shown to him by angels, saying that after the resurrection the Kingdom of Christ will be on earth and that the flesh, dwelling at Jerusalem, will again serve lusts and pleasures. And being an enemy of the writings of God, he, desirous to lead astray, says that there will be a season of a thousand years of marriage-festivity.

II. HISTORY OF THE NEW TESTAMENT BOOKS

LITERATURE

Edgar J. Goodspeed, *Introduction to the New Testament*, Chicago, 1937.
Caspar Rene Gregory, *Einleitung in das Neue Testament*, Leipzig, 1909.
Adolf von Harnack, *Beiträge zur Einleitung in das Neue Testament*, 4 Bände, Leipzig, 1906–1911.
Adolf Jülicher und Erich Fascher, *Einleitung in das Neue Testament*, 7. Auflage, (*Grundriss der theologischen Wissenschaften*, herausgegeben von Achelis, Bertholet et al., III, i), Tübingen, 1931.
Rudolf Knopf, *Einführung in das Neue Testament, Bibelkunde des Neuen Testaments, Geschichte und Religion des Urchristentums*, 4. Auflage (*Sammlung A. Töpelmann, Die Theologie im Anriss*: Band 2), Giessen, 1934.
Kirsopp and Silva Lake, *An Introduction to the New Testament*, New York and London, 1937.
P. M.-J. Lagrange, *Études Bibliques. Introduction à l'études du Nouveau Testament*, 4 Parties, Paris, 1933–1937.
Wilhelm Michaelis, *Einleitung in das Neue Testament. Die Entstehung, Sammlung und Überlieferung der Schriften des Neuen Testaments*, Bern, 1946.
James Moffatt, *An Introduction to the Literature of the New Testament* (*International Theological Library*), 3rd and revised ed., New York, reprinted 1927.
Burnett Hillman Streeter, *The Four Gospels, A Study of Origins treating the Manuscript Tradition, Sources, Authorship, and Dates*, 5th impression revised, London, 1936.
Theodor Zahn, *Einleitung in das Neue Testament*, 2 Bände, dritte, vielfach berichtigte und vervolständigte Auflage, Leipzig, 1906. English translation from the 3rd German edition under the direction and supervision of M. W. Jacobus, assisted by C. S. Thayer, *Introduction to the New Testament*, 3 vols., 2nd ed., Edinburgh, 1917.

Tatianus

28

Ὁ μέντοι γε πρότερος αὐτῶν ἀρχηγὸς ὁ Τατιανὸς συνάφειάν τινα καὶ συναγωγὴν οὐκ οἶδ' ὅπως τῶν εὐαγγελίων συνθείς, Τὸ διὰ τεσσάρων τοῦτο προσωνόμασεν, ὃ καὶ παρά τισιν εἰς ἔτι νῦν φέρεται· τοῦ δ' ἀποστόλου φασὶ τολμῆσαί τινας αὐτὸν μεταφράσαι φωνάς, ὡς ἐπιδιορθούμενον αὐτῶν τὴν τῆς φράσεως σύνταξιν.

Eusebius H.E. IV.29.6.

Fragmentum

29

[ζεβεδ]αίου καὶ σαλώμη κ[α]ὶ αἱ γυναῖκες[1]
[τῶν συ]νακολουθησάντων α[ὐτ]ῷ ἀπὸ τῆς
[γαλιλαί]ας ὁρῶσαι τὸν στα̅. ἦν δὲ[2]
[ἡ ἡμέρ]α παρασκευὴ σάββατον ἐπέφω
[σκεν ὀ]ψίας δὲ γενομένης ἐπὶ τ[ῇ π]αρασ[3]
[κευῇ] ὅ ἐστιν προσάββατον πρὸς
[ἦλθεν] ἄνθρωπος βουλευτη[ς ὑ]πάρ[4]
[χων ἀ]πὸ ἐρινμαθαία[ς] π[ό]λεως τῆς[5]
[ἰουδαί]ας ὄνομα ἰω[σὴφ] ἀ[γ]αθὸς δί[6]
[καιος] ὢν μαθητὴς [το]ῦ ιη̅. κα[τακε][7]
[κρυμ]μένος δὲ διὰ τὸν φόβον τῶν
[ἰουδαίω]ν καὶ αὐτὸς προσεδέχετο[8]
[τὴν] β[ασιλείαν] τοῦ θυ̅. οὗτος οὐκ[9]
[ἦν συνκατατ]ιθεμέν[ο]ς τῇ β[ουλῇ]

Le P. M.-J. Lagrange. *Critique textuelle* (*Introduction à l'étude du Noveau Testament*, II), p. 628.

[1]Mt. 27 : 56; Mk. 15 : 40; Lk. 23 : 49. [2]στα̅=σταυροῦντα, Lk. 23 : 54.
[3]Mt. 27 : 57; Mk. 15 : 42. [4]Mt. 27 : 57; Lk. 23 : 50. [5]Mt. 27 : 57; Lk. 23 : 51.
[6]Mt. 27 : 57; Lk. 23 : 50. [7]ιη̅=ιησοῦ, Jn. 19 : 38. [8]Mt. 27 : 57; Lk. 23 : 51b.
[9]θυ̅=θεοῦ, Lk. 23 : 51a.

A. The Four Gospels

1. TATIAN (*c*. A.D. 170)

28

Accordingly their former leader, Tatian, compiling a kind of unification and combination of the Gospels—I know not how—entitled it *The Diatessaron*. It is extant with some even until this day. And they say that he dared to paraphrase some of the Apostle's sayings, pretending to correct their syntax of language.

FRAGMENT

29

".... The mother of the sons of Zebedee *and Salome and the wives of those who had followed him from Galilee to see the crucified. And the day was Preparation; the Sabbath was dawning. And when it was evening, on the Pre*paration, *that is, the day before the Sabbath,* there came *up a man, being a member of the council, from Aramathea, a city of* Judea, *by name* Joseph, *good* and righteous, *being a disciple of Jesus, but secretly, for fear of the* Jews. *And he was looking for* the *kingdom of God. This man* had *not* consented *to* their *purpose*...."

Translation with the kind permission of Bruce M. Metzger, "Recently Published Papyri of the New Testament," *The Biblical Archaeologist*, Vol. X, 2 (May, 1947), pp. 43f.

Theodor Zahn, *Tatian's Diatessaron* (*Forschungen zur Geschichte des neutestamentlichen Kanons und der altkirchlichen Literatur*, herausgegeben von Th. Zahn, I. Theil), Erlangen und Leipzig, 1881; A. Hjelt, *Die altsyrische Evangelienübersetzung und Tatians Diatessaron besonders in ihrem gegenseitigen Verhältnis* (*Forschungen zur Geschichte des neutestamentlichen Kanons*, herausgegeben von Th. Zahn, VII. Theil. I. Heft) (Leipzig, 1903), pp. 16–75; Carl H. Kraeling, *A Greek Fragment of Tatian's Diatessaron from Dura* (*Studies and Documents*, ed. by Kirsopp and Silva Lake, 3), London, 1935; Curt Peters, *Das Diatessaron Tatians; seine Überlieferung und sein Nachwirken im Morgen- und Abendland sowie der heutige Stand seiner Erforschung*, Roma, 1939.

Irenaeus

30

Non enim per alios dispositionem salutis nostrae cognouimus, quam per eos, per quos euangelium peruenit ad nos; quod quidem tunc praeconauerunt, postea uero per Dei uoluntatem in Scripturis nobis tradiderunt, fundamentum et columnam fidei nostrae futurum. nec enim fas est dicere, quoniam ante praedicauerunt quam perfectam haberent agnitionem; sicut quidam audent dicere, gloriantes emendatores se esse apostolorum. postea enim quam surrexit Dominus noster a mortuis, et induti sunt superuenientis Spiritus sancti uirtutem ex alto, de omnibus adimpleti sunt et habuerunt perfectam agnitionem: exierunt in fines terrae, ea quae a Deo nobis bona sunt euangelizantes, et caelestem pacem hominibus annuntiantes, qui quidem et omnes pariter et singuli eorum habentes euangelium Dei.

Ὁ μὲν δὴ Ματθαῖος ἐν τοῖς Ἑβραίοις τῇ ἰδίᾳ αὐτῶν διαλέκτῳ καὶ γραφὴν ἐξήνεγκεν εὐαγγελίου, τοῦ Πέτρου καὶ τοῦ Παύλου ἐν Ῥώμῃ εὐαγγελιζομένων καὶ θεμελιούντων τὴν ἐκκλησίαν· μετὰ δὲ τὴν τούτων ἔξοδον Μάρκος, ὁ μαθητὴς καὶ ἑρμηνευτὴς Πέτρου, καὶ αὐτὸς τὰ ὑπὸ Πέτρου κηρυσσόμενα ἐγγράφως ἡμῖν παραδέδωκεν· καὶ Λουκᾶς δέ, ὁ ἀκόλουθος Παύλου, τὸ ὑπ' ἐκείνου κηρυσσόμενον εὐαγγέλιον ἐν βίβλῳ κατέθετο. ἔπειτα Ἰωάννης, ὁ μαθητὴς τοῦ κυρίου, ὁ καὶ ἐπὶ τὸ στῆθος αὐτοῦ ἀναπεσών, καὶ αὐτὸς ἐξέδωκεν τὸ εὐαγγέλιον, ἐν Ἐφέσῳ τῆς Ἀσίας διατρίβων.

Et omnes isti unum Deum factorem caeli et terrae, a lege et prophetis annuntiatum, et unum Christum filium Dei tradiderunt nobis; quibus si quis non assentit, spernit quidem participes Domini, spernit autem et ipsum Christum Dominum, spernit uero et Patrem, et est a semetipso damnatus, resistens et repugnans saluti suae; quod faciunt omnes haeretici.

Irenaeus *Adu. haer.* III.1.1-2, cf. Eusebius *H.E.* V.8.2.

2. GREEK AND LATIN FATHERS
IRENAEUS

30

a For we have learned the plan of our salvation through no others than through those through whom the Gospel has come down to us, which indeed they proclaimed at that time, but afterward by the will of God handed down to us in the Scriptures to be the foundation and pillar of our faith.[1] For it is not right to say that they preached before they had perfect knowledge, as certain dare to say, boasting that they are correctors of the Apostles. For after our Lord rose from the dead and when they were endued from on high with power of the Spirit who came upon them, they were filled with respect to all things and had perfect knowledge [and] went forth to the ends of the earth proclaiming those good things which are ours from God and announcing heavenly peace to men. All [of] them, indeed, both equally and each of them individually, possessed the Gospel of God.

b Now Matthew published also a book of the Gospel among the Hebrews in their own dialect, while Peter and Paul were preaching the Gospel in Rome and founding the Church. After their death,[2] Mark, the disciple and interpreter of Peter, he too handed down to us in writing the things preached by Peter. Luke also, the follower of Paul, put down in a book the Gospel preached by that one. Afterwards John, the disciple of the Lord who also leaned upon his breast, he too published a Gospel while residing in Ephesus [in] Asia.

And all these have handed down to us [the doctrine that there is] one God, maker of heaven and earth, proclaimed by the Law and the Prophets, and one Christ, the Son of God. If a person does not assent to these [doctrines], he surely rejects the followers of the Lord; he rejects even Christ the Lord himself; he rejects indeed also the Father and is self-condemned, resisting and fighting against his [own] salvation—which thing all the heretics do.

[1] Cf. I Tim. 3 : 15.   [2] Or "departure."
Hans Lietzmann, *Petrus und Paulus in Rom* (1915); H. Holstein, "La tradition des apostres chez Saint Irénée," *Recherches de science religieus*, 36 (1949), pp. 229-270.

Clemens Alexandrinus

31

Αὖθις δ' ἐν τοῖς αὐτοῖς ὁ Κλήμης βιβλίοις περὶ τῆς τάξεως τῶν εὐαγγελίων παράδοσιν τῶν ἀνέκαθεν πρεσβυτέρων τέθειται, τοῦτον ἔχουσαν τὸν τρόπον. προγεγράφθαι ἔλεγεν τῶν εὐαγγελίων τὰ περιέχοντα τὰς γενεαλογίας, τὸ δὲ κατὰ Μάρκον ταύτην ἐσχηκέναι τὴν οἰκονομίαν. τοῦ Πέτρου δημοσίᾳ ἐν Ῥώμῃ κηρύξαντος τὸν λόγον καὶ πνεύματι τὸ εὐαγγέλιον ἐξειπόντος, τοὺς παρόντας, πολλοὺς ὄντας, παρακαλέσαι τὸν Μάρκον, ὡς ἂν ἀκολουθήσαντα αὐτῷ πόρρωθεν καὶ μεμνημένον τῶν λεχθέντων, ἀναγράψαι τὰ εἰρημένα· ποιήσαντα δέ, τὸ εὐαγγέλιον μεταδοῦναι τοῖς δεομένοις αὐτοῦ· ὅπερ ἐπιγνόντα τὸν Πέτρον προτρεπτικῶς μήτε κωλῦσαι μήτε προτρέψασθαι. τὸν μέντοι Ἰωάννην ἔσχατον, συνιδόντα ὅτι τὰ σωματικὰ ἐν τοῖς εὐαγγελίοις δεδήλωται, προτραπέντα ὑπὸ τῶν γνωρίμων, πνεύματι θεοφορηθέντα πνευματικὸν ποιῆσαι εὐαγγέλιον.

Clemens Alexandrinus *Hyp.* cf. Eusebius *H.E.* VI.14.5.

Tertullianus

32

Constituimus imprimis euangelicum instrumentum apostolos auctores habere, quibus hoc munus euangelii promulgandi ab ipso domino sit impositum. si et apostolicos, non tamen solos, sed cum apostolis et post apostolos, quoniam praedicatio discipulorum suspecta fieri posset de gloriae studio, si non adsistat illi auctoritas magistrorum, immo Christi, quae magistros apostolos fecit. denique nobis fidem ex apostolis Iohannes et Matthaeus insinuant, ex apostolicis Lucas et Marcus instaurant isdem regulis exorsi, quantum ad unicum deum attinet creatorem et Christum eius, natum ex uirgine, supplementum legis et prophetarum.

Tertullianus *C. Marc.* IV.2.

CLEMENT OF ALEXANDRIA
(c. A. D. 150-203)

31

Again in the same books Clement gives a tradition of the early presbyters concerning the order of the Gospels in the following manner: He said that those Gospels which contain the genealogies were written first; but the [Gospel] according to Mark had this occasion: When Peter had preached the word publicly in Rome and had declared the Gospel by [the] Spirit, those who were present—they were many—besought Mark, since he had followed him (Peter) for a long time and remembered the things that had been spoken, to write out the things that had been said; and when he had done [this], he gave the Gospel to those who [had] asked him. When Peter learned of it later,[1] he neither obstructed nor commended [it]. Last of all, John, noticing that the physical things[2] had been set forth in the [other] Gospels, being urged by his companions and inspired by the Spirit, wrote a spiritual Gospel.

[1] The text is probably corrupt. The Latin version has *postmodum* which is followed here. Schwartz suggests πνευματικῶς, that is "by the Spirit" and refers to a similar statement in II, 15, 2.   [2] I.e. historical events.

TERTULLIAN (c. A. D. 155-222)

32

We lay it down first of all that the Evangelical instrument has Apostles as authors, upon whom this duty of promulgating the Gospel was laid by the Lord himself. And if [it be true that] there are also Apostolic men [among them], yet they are not alone but with Apostles and after Apostles, since the preaching of disciples could be suspected to be done because of a desire for glory, if the authority of the masters did not assist it, nay rather, [the authority] of Christ, which made the Apostles masters. So then, of Apostles, John and Matthew instill us with faith; of Apostolic men, Luke and Mark renew it, beginning with the same principles [of faith] so far as it pertains to one God, the creator, and his Christ, born of a virgin, the fulfillment of the Law and the Prophets.

33

Eadem auctoritas ecclesiarum apostolicarum ceteris quoque patrocinabitur euangeliis, quae proinde per illas et secundum illas habemus, Iohannis dico atque Matthei; licet et Marcus quod edidit Petri adfirmetur, cuius interpres Marcus. nam et Lucae digestum Paulo adscribere sólent; capit autem magistrorum uideri quae discipuli promulgarint.

Tertullianus C. Marc. IV.5.

Eusebius

34

Ὅμως δ' οὖν ἐξ ἁπάντων τῶν τοῦ κυρίου μαθητῶν ὑπομνήματα Ματθαῖος ἡμῖν καὶ Ἰωάννης μόνοι καταλελοίπασιν· οὓς καὶ ἐπάναγκες ἐπὶ τὴν γραφὴν ἐλθεῖν κατέχει λόγος. Ματθαῖός τε γὰρ πρότερον Ἑβραίοις κηρύξας, ὡς ἤμελλεν καὶ ἐφ' ἑτέρους ἰέναι, πατρίῳ γλώττῃ γραφῇ παραδοὺς τὸ κατ' αὐτὸν εὐαγγέλιον, τὸ λεῖπον τῇ αὐτοῦ παρουσίᾳ τούτοις ἀφ' ὧν ἐστέλλετο, διὰ τῆς γραφῆς ἀπεπλήρου· ἤδη δὲ Μάρκου καὶ Λουκᾶ τῶν κατ' αὐτοὺς εὐαγγελίων τὴν ἔκδοσιν πεποιημένων, Ἰωάννην φασὶ τὸν πάντα χρόνον ἀγράφῳ κεχρημένον κηρύγματι, τέλος καὶ ἐπὶ τὴν γραφὴν ἐλθεῖν τοιᾶσδε χάριν αἰτίας. τῶν προαναγραφέντων τριῶν εἰς πάντας ἤδη καὶ εἰς αὐτὸν διαδεδομένων, ἀποδέξασθαι μέν φασιν, ἀλήθειαν αὐτοῖς ἐπιμαρτυρήσαντα, μόνην δὲ ἄρα λείπεσθαι τῇ γραφῇ τὴν περὶ τῶν ἐν πρώτοις καὶ κατ' ἀρχὴν τοῦ κηρύγματος ὑπὸ τοῦ Χριστοῦ πεπραγμένων διήγησιν. καὶ ἀληθής γε ὁ λόγος. τοὺς τρεῖς γοῦν εὐαγγελιστὰς συνιδεῖν πάρεστιν μόνα τὰ μετὰ τὴν ἐν τῷ δεσμωτηρίῳ Ἰωάννου τοῦ βαπτιστοῦ κάθειρξιν ἐφ' ἕνα ἐνιαυτὸν πεπραγμένα τῷ σωτῆρι συγγεγραφότας αὐτό τε τοῦτ' ἐπισημηναμένους κατ' ἀρχὰς τῆς αὐτῶν ἱστορίας· μετὰ γοῦν τὴν τεσσαρακονταήμερον νηστείαν καὶ τὸν ἐπὶ ταύτῃ πειρασμὸν τὸν χρόνον τῆς ἰδίας γραφῆς ὁ μὲν Ματθαῖος δηλοῖ λέγων Ἀκούσας δὲ ὅτι Ἰωάννης παρεδόθη, ἀνεχώρησεν ἀπὸ τῆς Ἰουδαίας εἰς τὴν

33

The same authority of the Apostolic churches will afford protection to the other Gospels also, which we possess likewise through those [churches] and according to those [churches]—I mean [the Gospels] of John and also of Matthew; while what Mark edited, may be affirmed to be of Peter, whose interpreter Mark was. For Luke's " Gospel " " similarly " men are used to ascribe to Paul. And so it can be seen that the things which the disciples proclaimed, belonged to their masters.

EUSEBIUS (c. A. D. 270-340)

34

Yet, of all the disciples[1] of the Lord, only Matthew and John have left us [their] memoirs; and they, it is reported, had recourse to writing only [under pressure of] necessity. For Matthew, [who] preached earlier to Hebrews, when he was about to go to others also, committing his Gospel to writing in his native tongue, compensated by his writing for the loss of his presence to those from whom he was sent [away]. But when Mark and Luke had already published their Gospels, they say[2] that John, who the whole time had made use of unwritten preaching, finally resorted to writing also for the following reason: When the three previously written [Gospels] had already been delivered to all and to him, they say that [he] accepted [them], testifying to their truth, but [said] that there was likely lacking in the writing only the account of the things which were done by Christ during the first period and at the beginning of [His] preaching; and the statement is true. For one can[3] see that the three evangelists have recorded only the things which were done by the Saviour in the one year after the imprisonment of John the Baptist and that they indicate this very thing at the beginnings of their account[s]. For after the forty-day fasting and the temptation [following] thereupon, Matthew indicates the chronology in his own writing, saying[4]: " Now when he

---

[1]Following the variant in the text which reads μαθητῶν for διατριβῶν. The Latin version has, *ex discipulis* and the Syriac version, "Apostles."
[2]The indefinite plural which may be rendered: " men say," " it is said," or " it is reported."
[3]Impersonal singular, meaning: " it is present to " or " in the power of anyone."
[4]Mt. 4 : 12: " from Judaea " is wanting in the text of Matthew.

Γαλιλαίαν, ὁ δὲ Μάρκος ὡσαύτως Μετὰ δὲ τὸ παραδοθῆναι φησίν
Ἰωάννην ἦλθεν Ἰησοῦς εἰς τὴν Γαλιλαίαν, καὶ ὁ Λουκᾶς δὲ πρὶν
ἄρξασθαι τῶν τοῦ Ἰησοῦ πράξεων, παραπλησίως ἐπιτηρεῖ, φάσκων
ὡς ἄρα προσθεὶς Ἡρῴδης οἷς διεπράξατο πονηροῖς, κατέκλεισε
τὸν Ἰωάννην ἐν φυλακῇ. παρακληθέντα δὴ οὖν τούτων ἕνεκά φασι
τὸν ἀπόστολον Ἰωάννην τὸν ὑπὸ τῶν προτέρων εὐαγγελιστῶν
παρασιωπηθέντα χρόνον καὶ τὰ κατὰ τοῦτον πεπραγμένα τῷ
σωτῆρι (ταῦτα δ' ἦν τὰ πρὸ τῆς τοῦ βαπτιστοῦ καθείρξεως) τῷ
κατ' αὐτὸν εὐαγγελίῳ παραδοῦναι, αὐτό τε τοῦτ' ἐπισημήνασθαι,
τοτὲ μὲν φήσαντα Ταύτην ἀρχὴν ἐποίησεν τῶν παραδόξων ὁ
Ἰησους, τοτὲ δὲ μνημονεύσαντα τοῦ βαπτιστοῦ μεταξὺ τῶν Ἰησοῦ
πράξεων ὡς ἔτι τότε βαπτίζοντος ἐν Αἰνὼν ἐγγὺς τοῦ Σαλείμ,
σαφῶς τε τοῦτο δηλοῦν ἐν τῷ λέγειν Οὔπω γὰρ ἦν Ἰωάννης
βεβλημένος εἰς φυλακήν. οὐκοῦν ὁ μὲν Ἰωάννης τῇ τοῦ κατ' αὐτὸν
εὐαγγελίου γραφῇ τὰ μηδέπω τοῦ βαπτιστοῦ εἰς φυλακὴν βεβλημένου
πρὸς τοῦ Χριστοῦ πραχθέντα παραδίδωσιν, οἱ δὲ λοιποὶ τρεῖς
εὐαγγελισταὶ τὰ μετὰ τὴν εἰς τὸ δεσμωτήριον κάθειρξιν τοῦ
βαπτιστοῦ μνημονεύουσιν· οἷς καὶ ἐπιστήσαντι οὐκέτ' ἂν δόξαι
διαφωνεῖν ἀλλήλοις τὰ εὐαγγέλια τῷ τὸ μὲν κατὰ Ἰωάννην τὰ
πρῶτα τῶν τοῦ Χριστοῦ πράξεων περιέχειν, τὰ δὲ λοιπὰ τὴν ἐπὶ
τέλει τοῦ χρόνου αὐτῷ γεγενημένην ἱστορίαν· εἰκότως δ' οὖν τὴν
μὲν τῆς σαρκὸς τοῦ σωτῆρος ἡμῶν γενεαλογίαν ἅτε Ματθαίῳ καὶ
Λουκᾷ προγραφεῖσαν ἀποσιωπῆσαι τὸν Ἰωάννην, τῆς δὲ θεολογίας
ἀπάρξασθαι ὡς ἂν αὐτῷ πρὸς τοῦ θείου πνεύματος οἷα κρείττονι
παραπεφυλαγμένης. ταῦτα μὲν οὖν ἡμῖν περὶ τῆς τοῦ κατὰ Ἰωάννην
εὐαγγελίου γραφῆς εἰρήσθω, καὶ τῆς κατὰ Μάρκον δὲ ἡ γενομένη
αἰτία ἐν τοῖς πρόσθεν ἡμῖν δεδήλωται· ὁ δὲ Λουκᾶς ἀρχόμενος καὶ
αὐτὸς τοῦ κατ' αὐτὸν συγγράμματος τὴν αἰτίαν προύθηκεν δι' ἣν
πεποίηται τὴν σύνταξιν, δηλῶν ὡς ἄρα πολλῶν καὶ ἄλλων προπετέσ-
τερον ἐπιτετηδευκότων διήγησιν ποιήσασθαι ὧν αὐτὸς πεπληρο-
φόρητο λόγων, ἀναγκαίως ἀπαλλάττων ἡμᾶς τῆς περὶ τοὺς ἄλλους
ἀμφηρίστου ὑπολήψεως, τὸν ἀσφαλῆ λόγον ὧν αὐτὸς ἱκανῶς τὴν
ἀλήθειαν κατειλήφει ἐκ τῆς ἅμα Παύλῳ συνουσίας τε καὶ διατριβῆς
καὶ τῆς τῶν λοιπῶν ἀποστόλων ὁμιλίας ὠφελημένος, διὰ τοῦ ἰδίου
παρέδωκεν εὐαγγελίου.

Eusebius H.E. III.24.5–15.

heard that John was delivered up, he withdrew from Judaea into Galilee;" and Mark likewise says:[1] "After John was delivered up, Jesus went into Galilee;" and Luke also, before beginning the deeds of Jesus, makes an almost similar observation by saying[2] that Herod, adding to the crimes that he had perpetrated, shut up John in prison. They say that, when he had been called upon for these reasons, the Apostle John handed down in his Gospel [an account of] the time passed over in silence by the former evangelists and [of] the things which were done at this time by the Saviour—and these were the things [which happened] before the imprisonment of the Baptist; and that he signifies this very thing, on one occasion saying[3]: "This first of miracles Jesus did...," and that, on another [occasion], mentioning the Baptist in the midst of [an account] of the deeds of Jesus as still at that time baptizing in Aenon near Salim[4], he clearly shows this by saying[5]: "For John had not yet been cast into prison." Therefore, John, in the text of his Gospel, hands down the things done by Christ when the Baptist was not yet cast into prison; but the other three evangelists tell of the things [done] after the imprisonment of the Baptist. And to one who understands these things the Gospels would no longer seem to disagree with one another, since the [Gospel] according to John contains the first of the deeds of Christ, but the others [contain] a narrative [of the things] done by Him at the end of the period. It is natural, therefore, that John kept silence concerning the genealogy of the human nature[6] of our Saviour, because [this had been] previously recorded by Matthew and Luke, but began with [an account of] His deity[7], since this had been reserved by the divine Spirit for him—as it were for a superior [one]. Let these things, then, concerning the writing of the Gospel of John suffice us. And the occasion of the Gospel of Mark has been shown to us above; but Luke, at the outset[8] stated himself the reason why he made his account, by showing how many others had, with too much haste, made a practice of producing written narrative[s] of the things of which he himself had full knowledge, [and judging it] necessary to liberate us from the unreliable opinions of the others, he handed down [to us] in his own Gospel the reliable account of the things whose truth he had well learned with the help of his association and sojourn with Paul and his converse with the other Apostles.

---

[1] Mk. 1 : 14. [2] Lk. 3 : 20. [3] Jn. 2 : 11. [4] Jn. 3 : 23. [5] Jn. 3 : 24. [6] Literally "flesh."
[7] Literally "the theology," but used in the above sense in the time of Eusebius; translated in II, 1, 1 by *de divinitate salvatoris*.   [8] Lk. 1 : 1-4.

Prologi Quattuor Euangeliorum

35

Plures fuisse qui euangelia scripserunt, et Lucas euangelista testatur dicens Quoniam quidem multi conati sunt ordinare narrationem rerum, quae in nobis completae sunt, sicut tradiderunt nobis qui ab initio ipsi uiderunt sermonem et ministrauerunt ei, et perseuerantia usque ad praesens tempus monumenta declarant, quae a diuersis auctoribus edita, diuersarum haeresium fuere principia, ut est illud iuxta Aegyptios et Thomam et Matthiam et Bartholomeum duodecim quoque apostolorum et Basilidis atque Apellis ac reliquorum, quos enumerare longissimum est, cum hoc tantum in praesentiarum necesse sit dicere, extitisse quosdam, qui sine spiritu et gratia dei conati sunt magis ordinare narrationem, quam historiae texere ueritatem. quibus iure potest illud propheticum coaptari Uae qui prophetant de corde suo, qui ambulant post spiritum suum, qui dicunt, "dicit dominus" et dominus non misit eos, de quibus et saluator in euangelio Iohannis loquitur Omnes qui ante me uenerunt fures fuerunt et latrones: qui uenerunt, non qui missi sunt; ipse enim ait Ueniebant et ego non mittebam eos. in uenientibus praesumptio temeritatis, in missis obsequium ueritatis est. ecclesia autem, quae supra petram domini fundata est, quam introduxit rex in cubiculum suum et ad quam per foramen descensionis occulte misit manum suam, similis dammulae hinnuloque ceruorum, quattuor flumina paradisi instar eructans, quattuor et angulos et annullos habet, per quos quasi arca testimenti et custos legis domini lignis mobilibus uehitur.

JEROME (A. D. c. 340–420)
Prologues to the Four Gospels from his commentary on Matthew

35

a   Luke, the Evangelist, also testifies that there have been many who wrote Gospels, saying: " For many, indeed, have attempted to draw up a narrative of the things which have been fulfilled among us, even as they, who themselves have been eyewitnesses and ministers of the Word from the beginning, have handed it down to us ",[1] and up to the present time they are declaring with perseverance the records which have been published by diverse authors as the beginnings of diverse heresies: as, for instance, " those " [Gospels] according to the Egyptians and [according to] Thomas and Matthias and Bartholomew, and also [that] of the twelve Apostles and of both Basilides and Apelles and of the rest,
b which to enumerate is too long, since presently this only would be necessary to state, that there existed some who have attempted, without the Spirit and grace of God, to draw up a story rather than to defend the truth of history. To them that prophetic [statement] can rightly be applied: "Alas! they prophesy out of their own heart, they follow after their own spirit, they say: ' The Lord says,' but the Lord did not send them;"[2] about them also the Redeemer speaks in the Gospel of John: "All who came before me were thieves and robbers;"[3] they came who have not been sent. For he himself affirms: " They came, but I did not send them."[4] Rash presumption[5] among those who are coming is yielding of truth among those who have been sent. The Church, however, which is founded on the rock of the Lord, whom the King has led into His sleeping-chamber, and to whom He has stretched His hand secretly through the orifice[6] of His descent, similar to a roe and young hart of the horned creatures, producing four rivers according to the likeness of Paradise, has both four corners and four rings through which it is carried like the Ark of the Covenant and the receptacle of the Law of the Lord with loose bars.

---

[1] Lk. 1 : 1ff.   [2] Ez. 13 : 3, 6.   [3] John 10 : 8.   [4] Cf. Jer 14 : 14; 27 : 15.
[5] Literally " The presumption of rashness."
[6] It may be an allusion to Song of Sol. 5 : 4.

Mattheus

36

Primus omnium Mattheus est publicanus cognomento Leui, qui euangelium in Iudaea hebreo sermone edidit ob eorum uel maxime causam, qui in Iesum crediderant ex Iudaeis et nequaquam legis umbra succedente euangelii ueritatem seruabant.

Marcus

37

Secundus Marcus, interpres apostoli Petri et Alexandrinae ecclesiae primus episcopus, qui dominum quidem saluatorem ipse non uidit, sed ea quae magistrum audierat praedicantem iuxta fidem magis gestorum narrauit, quam ordinem.

Lucas

38

Tertius Lucas medicus natione Syrus Antiochensis, cuius laus in euangelio, qui et ipse discipulus apostoli Pauli in Achaiae Boeotiaeque partibus uolumen condidit, quaedam altius repetens, et ut ipse in prooemio confitetur, audita magis, quam uisa describens.

Iohannes

39

Ultimus Iohannes apostolus et euangelista, quem Iesus amauit plurimum, qui super pectus domini recumbens purissima doctrinarum fluenta potauit et qui solus de cruce meruit audire Ecce mater tua. is cum esset in Asia et iam tunc haereticorum semina pullularent, Cerinthi, Hebionis et ceterorum, qui negant Christum in carne uenisse, quos et ipse in epistula sua antichristos uocat et apostolus Paulus fre-

MATTHEW

36

Matthew, the publican with the cognomen Levi, is the first of all who published a Gospel in Judaea in the Hebrew language, especially for the sake of those out of the Jews who had believed in Jesus and [who] were observing the truth of the Gospel while the shadow of the law had in no wise disappeared.

MARK

37

Mark, the interpreter of the Apostle Peter, and the first bishop of the church of Alexandria, who himself has not seen the Lord, the very Saviour, is the second [who published a Gospel], but he narrated those things, which he had heard [his] master preaching, more in accordance with the trustworthiness of the things performed than [in accordance with their] sequence.

LUKE

38

Luke, the physician, by nation a Syrian of Antioch, whose glory was in the Gospel, who was himself also a follower of the Apostle Paul, investigating some things more profoundly, and describing the things which were heard rather than the things which were seen, as he himself also admits in the prologue, is the third [who] compiled a volume in the regions of Achaea and Boeotia.

JOHN

39

Last is John, the Apostle and Evangelist, whom Jesus loved most, who, reclining on the breast of the Lord, drank the purest streams of teachings and who alone merited to hear from the cross: " Behold, thy mother."[1] He—when he was in Asia, and at that time the seeds of the heretics, Cerinthus, Ebion, and others, who deny that Christ came in the flesh, whom he himself

[1] Jn. 19 : 27.

quenter percutit, coactus est ab omnibus paene tunc Asiae episcopis et multarum ecclesiarum legationibus de diuinitate saluatoris altius scribere et ad ipsum, ut ita dicam, dei uerbum non tam audaci, quam felici temeritate prorumpere, ut ecclesiastica narrat historia. cum a fratribus cogeretur, ut scriberet, ita facturum respondisse, si indicto ieiunio in communi omnes deum deprecarentur; quo expleto reuelatione saturatus in illud prooemium caelo ueniens eructavit In principio erat uerbum et uerbum erat apud deum et deus erat hoc uerbum: hoc erat in principio apud deum.

Ex *commentario S. Hieronymi in Mattheum.*

J. Wordsworth and H. I. White, *Nouum Testamentum Domini Nostri Jesu Christi Latine* (Oxford, 1889–1908), I, pp. 11–13.

Augustinus

40

Horum sane quattuor solus Mattheus Hebraeo scripsisse perhibetur eloquio, ceteri Graeco. et quamuis singuli suum quendam narrandi ordinem tenuisse uideantur, non tamen unusquisque eorum uelut alterius preacedentis ignarus uoluisse scribere repperitur uel ignorante preatermisisse, quae scripsisse alius inuenitur, sed sicut unicuique inspiratum est non superfluam cooperationem sui laboris adiunxit. nam Mattheus suscepisse intellegitur incarnationem domini secundum stirpem regiam et pleraque secundum hominum praesentem uitam facta et dicta eius. Marcus eum subsecutus tamquam pedisequus et breuiator eius uidetur. cum solo quippe Iohanne nihil dixit, solus ipse perpauca, cum solo Luca pauciora, cum Mattheo uero plurima et multa paene totidem adque ipsis uerbis siue cum solo siue cum ceteris consonante. Lucas autem circa sacerdotalem domini stirpem adque personam magis occupatus apparet.

Augustinus *De consensu euangelistarum* I.2.4.

also calls Antichrists in his epistle and [at whom] the Apostle Paul frequently lashes out, were already shooting up—he was urged by almost all the bishops of Asia at that time and by delegates of many churches to write more profoundly about the divinity of the Saviour and, so to speak, to break through to the very Word of God—not so much with boldness as with fortunate[1] haste, as the *Ecclesiastical History* relates. When he was urged by the brethren to write, [he is said] to have replied that he would do so, if, when a general fast had been proclaimed, all would pray to God. When it was carried out, saturated with revelation, he burst forth into that heaven-sent prologue: " In the beginning was the Word, and the Word was with God, and this Word was God. The same was in the beginning with God."[2]

[1] Fortunately in the light of the fact that John died shortly afterwards. [2] Jn. 1 : 1.

AUGUSTIN (A. D. 354-430)

40

Of these four, it is certain, only Matthew is regarded to have written in the Hebrew language, the others in Greek. And although they may create the impression that each [of them] kept a certain individual order of narration, yet it is not to be taken as if any one of them chose to write [in] ignorance of his predecessor, or to have left out things which another is found to have recorded, [as if] they were unknown [to him]; but as each was inspired he did not add superfluous " common material " [to] his work. For Matthew is assumed to have undertaken [the narrative of] the incarnation of the Lord " emphasizing " [His] regal descent and especially [His] deeds and sayings as they pertain to the present life of men. Mark followed him closely and looks like his imitator and epitomizer. "Compared separately " with John, as one might expect, he said nothing in common. [Nevertheless he said] very little on his own: " Compared separately " with Luke [he said] rather little [on his own]; but " compared " with Matthew [he said] very much, and many things in almost exactly the same way and even with the same words, either with him alone[1] or with the others. Luke, however, appears to have been occupied mostly with the priestly lineage and nature of the Lord.

[1] I.e. Matthew.

Prologi Monarchiani

41

Incipit argumentum euangelii secundum Mattheum

Mattheus ex Iudaea[1] sicut in ordine primus ponitur, ita euangelium in Iudaea primus scripsit. cuius uocatio ad deum[2] ex publicanis actibus fuit. duorum in generatione Christi principia praesumens, unius cuius prima circumcisio in carne, alterius cuius secundum cor electio fuit, et ex utrisque in patribus Christus, sicque quaternario denario numero triformiter posito, principium a credendi fide in electionis tempus porrigens et ex electione in transmigrationis diem dirigens atque a transmigratione usque in[3] Christum definiens decursam aduentus domini ostendit generationem, ut et numero satisfaciens et tempori et se quod esset ostendens et dei in se opus monstrans, etiam in his, quorum genus posuit, Christi operantis a principio testimonium non negaret. quarum omnium rerum tempus, ordo, numerus, dispositio, uel ratio, quod fidei necessarium est, deus Christus est, qui factus ex muliere, factus sub lege, natus ex uirgine, passus in carne omnia in cruce fixit, ut triumphans ea in semetipso, resurgens in corpore, et patris nomen in patribus filio et filii nomen patri restitueret in filiis, sine principio, sine fine, ostendens unum se cum patre esse, quia unus est. in quo euangelio utile est desiderantibus deum sic prima uel media uel perfecta cognoscere, ut et uocationem apostoli et opus euangelii et dilectionem dei in carne nascentis per uniuersa legentes intellegant atque id in eo, in quo adprehensi sunt et adprehendere expetunt, recognoscant. nobis enim hoc in studio argumenti fuit, et fidem factae rei tradere et operantis dei intellegendam diligenter esse dispositionem quaerentibus non tacere.

Explicit argumentum euangelii secundum Mattheum

[1]Chapman: Iudaeis.   [2]Chapman: ad Dominum.   [3]Chapman: ad.

3. MONARCHIAN PROLOGUES

41

Here begins the argument of the Gospel according to Matthew

a   Matthew, from Judaea, just as he is placed first in order, so he also wrote [his] Gospel first in Judaea. He " was called " to God from [his] publican activities. Assuming double origins in the generation of Christ, the first one of which was the circumcision in the flesh, the second of which was the election according to the heart—and by both of these Christ was in [his] ancestors,—and thus, having set down thrice the number fourteen, " tracing " [his] beginning from the faith of the believer[1] to the time of the election[2], and " proceeding " from the election to the time of the migration [to Babylon], and drawing it up from the migration to Christ, he shows the completed generation of the advent of the Lord so that, doing justice to both the number and the time, and
b   showing what he was and exhibiting God's work in himself, he did not deny the witness of Christ [who] was working from the beginning even in those whose genealogy he put down. The time, the order, the number, the arrangement, and the reason of all these things—which " are " necessary for faith[3], namely God is Christ, who was " born " of a woman, made under the law[4], born of a virgin, suffered in the flesh, nailed all things to the cross in order that, triumphing over them in Himself[5], rising again in the body, He might both restore the name of father in the fathers to the Son, and the name of son to the Father in the sons, [who is] without beginning, without end, showing Himself to be one with the Father,[6] because He is one [with Him].

In this Gospel it is profitable for those who are yearning for God, so to become acquainted with the " beginning " and the " middle " and the " end " that, reading through the whole [book], they may understand both the calling of the Apostle and the work of the Gospel, and the Love of God, born in the flesh, and that they may also come to know in it that in which they were apprehended and expect to apprehend. For in the composition (?) of the preface it was our [intention] not to keep silent, but to hand down the truth of the matter and to make known to those who investigate that the orderly manner of God at work, is worthy of " diligent " learning.

Here ends the argument of the Gospel according to Matthew

---

[1] Chapman: Abraham. [2] Chapman: David. [3] I.e. to believe.
[4] Gal. 4 : 4. [5] Cf. Col. 2, 14f. [6] Jn. 10 : 30.

42

Incipit argumentum euangelii secundum Iohannem

Hic est Iohannes euangelista unus ex discipulis dei, qui uirgo electus a deo est, quem de nuptiis uolentem nubere uocauit deus. cui uirginitatis in hoc duplex testimonium in euangelio datur, quod et prae ceteris dilectus a deo dicitur et huic matrem suam iens ad crucem commendauit deus, ut uirginem uirgo seruaret. denique manifestans in euangelio quod erat ipse incorruptibilis, uerbi opus inchoans solus uerbum caro factum esse nec lumen a tenebris comprehensum fuisse testatur, primum signum ponens quod in nuptiis fecit deus, ut ostendens quod erat ipse legentibus demonstraret, quod ubi dominus inuitatur deficere nuptiarum uinum debeat ac[1] ueteribus immutatis noua omnia, quae a Christo instituuntur, adpareant. de quo singula quaeque in mysterio acta uel dicta euangelii ratio quaerentibus monstrat. hoc autem euangelium scripsit in Asia, posteaquam in Pathmos insula apocalypsin scripserat, ut cui in principio canonis incorruptibile principium in Genesi, et incorruptibilis finis per uirginem in apocalypsi redderetur dicente Christo Ego sum A et Ω. et hic est Iohannes, qui sciens superuenisse diem recessus sui conuocatis discipulis suis in Epheso per multa signorum experimenta promens Christum descendens in defossum sepulturae suae locum facta oratione positus est ad patres suos tam extraneus a dolore mortis, quam a corruptione carnis inuenitur alienus. qui et si[2] post omnes euangelium scripsisse dicitur, tam et[3] dispositione canonis ordinati post Mattheum ponitur, quoniam in domino quae nouissima sunt non uelut extrema et abiecta numero, sed plenitudinis opere perfecta sunt, et hoc uirgini debebatur. quorum tamen uel scripturarum tempore dispositio uel librorum ordinatio ideo per singula a nobis non exponitur, ut sciendi desiderio conlocato et quaerentibus fructus laboris et deo magisterii doctrina seruetur.

Explicit argumentum euangelii secundum Iohannem

[1]Chapman: ut.   [2]Substituted for etsi.   [3]Substituted for tamen

---

[1]Corssen and Chapman prefer to take *incorruptibilis* with *verbi*, but *a corruptione... alienus* further down corroborates the translation given above as Preuschen also seems to accept.
[2]Rev. 1 : 8, 21 : 6, 22 : 13.   [3]Literally: "so he is also."

42

Here begins the argument of the Gospel according to John

a This is John, the Evangelist, one of the disciples of God, who was chosen by God as a virgin, whom God called from marriage when he was intending [to wed.] To this effect a double testimony of [his] virginity is given to him in [his] Gospel, both that he is said [to have been] loved by God above the others and [that] God, when going to the cross, commended His mother to him so that a virgin might serve the Virgin. Further, showing in the Gospel that he himself was incorruptible[1] [and] beginning the work of the Word, he alone testifies that the Word was made flesh and that the light was not comprehended by the darkness; recording the first sign that God did at the wedding, in order that, showing what He indeed was, he might demonstrate to the readers, that, where the Lord is invited, the wine of the nuptials ought to fail and, the old having been changed, all things which are instituted by Christ, may appear new. Regarding this, the "purpose" of the Gospel [is to] show each thing, which was done or said in a
b mystery, to those who seek. Further, he wrote this Gospel in Asia, after he had written the Apocalypse in the island of Patmos, in order that to whom the incorruptible beginning was ascribed in the beginning of the canon in Genesis, to Him also the incorruptible end might be attributed [employing] a virgin [as His instrument], since Christ said: "I am the Alpha and the Omega."[2]

And this is John, who, when he realized that the day of his departure had come, when his disciples had been called together in Ephesus, while he presented Christ with many "examples" of signs, [and] descended into the place dugged out for his sepulture, was gathered to his fathers, when prayer had been offered, as free from the anguish of death as he was found foreign to corruption of the flesh.

And if he is said to have written [his] Gospel last of all, he is accordingly[3] placed after Matthew in the arrangement of the ordered canon. [But this does not matter] since with the Lord the things that are latest are not as if [they are] last and despicable by order, but they have been perfected by the work of fulness; and this was due to the virgin. The arrangement, however, either of their writings in time, or the order of [their] books, is, therefore, not explained by us in detail in order that, when the desire [to] know [it] has been stimulated, both the fruit of labor may be preserved for those who inquire and the office of instruction for God.

Here ends the argument of the Gospel according to John

43

Incipit argumentum euangelii secundum Lucam

Lucas Syrus natione Antiochensis, arte medicus, discipulus apostolorum, postea Paulum secutus usque ad confessionem eius seruiens deo sine crimine. nam neque uxorem umquam habens neque filios LXXIIII annorum obiit in Bithynia plenus spiritu sancto. qui cum iam descripta essent euangelia per Mattheum quidem in Iudaea, per Marcum autem in Italia, sancto instigante spiritu in Achaiae partibus hoc scripsit euangelium, significans etiam ipse in principio ante alia esse descripta. cui extra ea quae ordo euangelicae dispositionis exposcit, ea maxime necessitas laboris fuit, ut primum Graecis fidelibus omni perfectione uenturi in carnem dei manifestata, ne Iudaicis fabulis intenti in solo legis desiderio tenerentur neue hereticis fabulis et stultis sollicitationibus seducti excederent a ueritate elaboraret, dehinc ut in principio euangelii Iohannis natiuitate praesumpta cui euangelium scriberet et in quo electus scriberet indicaret, contestans in se completa esse, quae essent ab aliis inchoata. cui ideo post baptismum filii dei a perfectione generationis in Christo impletae et repetendae a principio natiuitatis humanae potestas permissa est, ut requirentibus demonstraret, in quo adprehendens erat, per Nathan filium introitu recurrentis in deum generationis admisso indispartibilis deus praedicans in hominibus Christum suum perfecti opus hominis redire in se per filium facere, qui per Dauid patrem uenientibus iter praebebat in Christo. cui Lucae non immerito etiam scribendorum apostolicorum actuum potestas in ministerio datur, ut deo in deum pleno ac filio proditionis extincto oratione ab apostolis facta sorte domini electionis numerus compleretur sicque Paulus consummationem apostolicis actibus daret, quem diu contra

43

Here begins the argument of the Gospel according to Luke

a   Luke of Antioch, a Syrian by nation, by profession a physician, a disciple of the Apostles, afterwards followed Paul until his confession[1], serving God without blame. For never having either a wife or "children," he died in Bithynia seventy-four years old, filled with the Holy Spirit. When the Gospels had already been written, on the one hand, by Matthew in Judaea, on the other hand, by Mark in Italy, he, under inspiration of the Holy Spirit, wrote this Gospel in the regions of Achaea. He too indicates in the beginning that others had been written before. Apart from what the evangelical plan of salvation demands, the inevitable course of his toil was primarily that he should work first among the Greek believers, lest, after all the fulness of God coming in the flesh had been made manifest, they, intent on
b   Jewish fables, would be captivated by the yearning for the law only, or lest, led astray by heretical fables and foolish questions, would depart from the truth; further, that in the beginning of [his] Gospel, after he had given the nativity of John, he might indicate to whom he wrote [his] Gospel and the purpose of his choice [to] write, contending that what was begun by others was completed by him. To him, therefore, ability was granted to trace [the history] after the baptism of the Son of God, from the completion of the generation fulfilled and repeated in Christ and from the beginning of [His] human nativity, that he might show to those who investigate—in so far he himself had apprehended—that—by admitting [into the list] an entry of the genealogy which runs back through the son of Nathan to God—the indivisible God, proclaiming His Christ among men, [has] made the work of the perfect man to revert to Himself through the Son—He who furnished through David, the father, a way in Christ for those who came [to Him].

On this Luke, not immeritorious, was bestowed ministerial ability also [to] write the Acts of the Apostles that, when God had been made complete[2] in God and the son of perdition annihilated, after prayer had been made by the Apostles, the number of election might be supplemented by the lot of the Lord, and that thus Paul, whom the Lord had chosen while he was kicking against the pricks[3] for a long time, might supply the consummation to the Acts of the Apostles.

---

[1] I.e. Paul's martyrdom.   [2] I.e. through the ascension   [3] Acts 26 : 14.

stimulos recalcitrantem dominus elegisset. Quod legentibus ac requirentibus deum etsi per singula expediri a nobis utile fuerat, scientes tamen, quod operantem agricolam oporteat de fructibus suis edere, uitauimus publicam curiositatem ne non tam uolentibus deum uideremur quam fastidientibus prodidisse.

Explicit argumentum euangelii secundum Lucam

44

Incipit argumentum euangelii secundum Marcum

Marcus euangelista dei et Petri in baptismate filius atque in diuino sermone discipulus sacerdotium in Israhel agens secundum carnem leuita, conuersus ad fidem Christi euangelium in Italia scripsit ostendens in eo, quod et generi suo deberet et Christo. nam initium principii in uoce propheticae exclamationis instituens ordinem leuiticae electionis ostendit, ut praedicans praedestinatum Iohannem filium Zachariae in uoce angeli adnuntiantis, non emissum solum uerbum caro factum sed corpus domini in omnia per uerbum diuinae uocis animatum initio euangelicae praedicationis ostenderet, ut qui haec legens sciret, cui initium carnis in domino et dei aduenientis habitaculum caro deberet agnoscere, atque in se uerbum uocis, quod in consonantibus perdiderat, inueniret. denique et perfecti euangelii opus intrans et a baptismo domini praedicare deum inchoans non laborauit natiuitatem carnis, quam in prioribus uiderat, dicere, sed totus inprimis expulsionem deserti, ieiunium numeri, temptationem diaboli, congregationem bestiarum et ministerium protulit angelorum, ut instituens nos ad intellegendum singula in breui compingens nec auctoritatem factae rei demeret et

Although it had been useful that this be explained by us in detail for those who are reading and seeking God, nevertheless, knowing that the laboring husbandman ought to eat of his fruits, we have avoided public curiosity lest we should appear to have made God known not so much to those who desire as to those who loathe [Him].

Here ends the argument of the Gospel according to Luke

44
Here begins the argument of the Gospel according to Mark

a   Mark, an Evangelist of God and by baptism the son of Peter and also his disciple in the divine word, exercising the priesthood in Israel, being a Levite according to the flesh, after he had been converted to the faith of Christ, wrote a Gospel in Italy pointing out in it for what he was indebted to his ancestry and for what to Christ. For composing the introduction of the beginning [of his Gospel] with the voice of the prophet's cry, he showed the purpose of [his] Levitical election so that he—declaring by the voice of the heralding messenger that John, the son of Zacharias, [was] the predestinated one[1]—might point out at the beginning of the narration of the "Gospel" that the Word, made flesh, had not only been sent out, but that, through the word of the divine voice the body of the Lord had been diffused into all things, in order that the one who reads these things might know to acknowledge to whom he was indebted for the beginning of the flesh in the Lord and the tabernacle of God coming as flesh, and also that he might find in himself the word of the voice which
b   had been lost in consonants.[2] Thereupon, both proceeding with the Gospel proper and essaying that God preached from the baptism of the Lord on, he did not take trouble to mention the nativity of the flesh, which he had noticed in the earlier [Gospels] but right at the beginning mentioned the expulsion "into" the desert, the fasting "for" the number [of days], the temptation of the devil, the gathering of the wild beasts, and the ministering of the angels, that, while "bringing" us to understand by sketching each event in brief, he might not lessen the authority

---

[1] The author seems to infer from Mk. 1 : 2ff. that John the Baptist was Elijah, cf. Mal. 4 : 5; Mk. 9 : 11f.
[2] In the incarnation the divine nature seems to have been regarded as the soul, the vowel. The body was the consonants. Thus consonants and vowel constitute the Word, cf. Chapman, p. 236.

perficiendo operi plenitudinem non negaret. denique amputasse sibi post fidem pollicem dicitur, ut sacerdotio reprobus haberetur, sed tantum consentiens fidei praedestinata potuit electio, ut nec sic in opere verbi perderet, quod prius meruerat in genere: nam Alexandriae episcopus fuit. cuius per singula opus scire et euangelii in se dicta disponere et disciplinam in se legis agnoscere et divinam in carne domini intellegere naturam. quae et nos primum requiri, dehinc inquisita uolumus agnosci, habentes mercedem exhortationis quoniam qui plantat et qui rigat unum sunt, qui autem incrementum praestat, deus est.

Explicit argumentum euangelii secundum Marcum

Erwin Preuschen. *Analecta (Sammlung ausgewählter kirchen- und dogmengeschichtlicher Quellenschriften*, Erste Reihe, Achtes Heft, 11) (Tübingen, 1910), pp. 89–93.

Papais

45

Ματθαῖος μὲν οὖν Ἑβραΐδι διαλέκτῳ τὰ λόγια συνετάξατο[1], ἡρμήνευσεν δ' αὐτὰ ὡς ἦν δυνατὸς ἕκαστος.

Papias, cf. Eusebius *H.E.* III.39.16.

[1]Variant συνεγράψατο.

Pantaenus Alexandrinus

46

Ὧν εἷς γενόμενος καὶ ὁ Πάνταινος, καὶ εἰς Ἰνδοὺς ἐλθεῖν λέγεται, ἔνθα λόγος εὑρεῖν αὐτὸν προφθάσαν τὴν αὐτοῦ παρουσίαν τὸ κατὰ Ματθαῖον εὐαγγέλιον παρά τισιν αὐτόθι τὸν Χριστὸν ἐπεγνωκόσιν,

of the work [already] done [in the earlier Gospels], and might not deny the work, [which was yet] to be completed,[1] its fulness. Further, he is said to have amputated his thumb after he [had embraced] the faith, that he might be accounted unfit for the priesthood, but the predestinated election, concurring with [his] faith, so prevailed that he did not lose in the ministry of the Word, what he had merited formerly in ancestry; for he was Alexandria's bishop whose task [it was] to know in detail and to apply the precepts of the Gospel on his own, and to know the discipline of the law on his own, and to understand the divine nature of the Lord in the flesh; these things we also desire to be searched for first, and, thereupon, when they have been searched for, to be understood, having the reward of the exhortation that "He who plants and he who waters are one, but the one who yields increase is God."[2]

Here ends the argument of the Gospel according to Mark

[1] I.e. Mark's own Gospel. [2] Cf. I Cor. 3 : 7f.
Peter Corssen, *Monarchianische Prologe zu den vier Evangelien* (*T. u. U.*, XV. Band, Heft 1), 1897; John Chapman, *Notes on the Early History of the Vulgate Gospels* (Oxford, 1908), pp. 218–253; Erwin Preuschen, *loc. cit.*; Robert M. Grant, "The Oldest Gospel Prologues," *Anglican Theological Review*, 22–23 (1940–1941), pp. 231–245.

B. The Gospel of Matthew

PAPIAS

45

Then Matthew "wrote" the oracles in [the] Hebrew dialect,[1] but everyone interpreted[2] them as he was able.

[1] Or "language." [2] Or "translated."
The Oracles ascribed to Matthew by Papias of Hierapolis, A Contribution to the Criticism of the New Testament (Anonymous), London, 1894.

PANTAENUS OF ALEXANDRIA (c. A. D. 180)

46

Pantaenus also was one of them and [is] said to have gone to India, where the story [goes] that he found the Gospel according to Matthew, [which] had preceded his arrival, among certain

οἷς Βαρθολομαῖον τῶν ἀποστόλων ἕνα κηρῦξαι αὐτοῖς τε· Ἑβραίων γράμμασι τὴν τοῦ Ματθαίου καταλεῖψαι γραφήν, ἣν καὶ σώζεσθαι εἰς τὸν δηλούμενον χρόνον.

Eusebius *H.E.* V.10.3, cf. Hieronymus *De uir. inl.* XXXVI.

Hieronymus

47

Matthaeus qui et Leui, ex publicano apostolus, primus in Judaea, propter eos qui ex circumcisione crediderunt, euangelium Christi Hebraeis litteris uerbisque conposuit; quod quis postea in Graecum transtulerit, non satis certum est.

Hieronymus *De uir. inl.* III, cf. *Prolog. in Matt.* (*no.* 40 *supra*).

Papias

48

Καὶ τοῦθ' ὁ πρεσβύτερος ἔλεγεν Μάρκος μὲν ἑρμηνευτὴς Πέτρου γενόμενος, ὅσα ἐμνημόνευσεν, ἀκριβῶς ἔγραψεν, οὐ μέντοι τάξει τὰ ὑπὸ τοῦ κυρίου ἢ λεχθέντα ἢ πραχθέντα. οὔτε γὰρ ἤκουσεν τοῦ κυρίου οὔτε παρηκολούθησεν αὐτῷ, ὕστερον δέ, ὡς ἔφην, Πέτρῳ· ὃς πρὸς τὰς χρείας ἐποιεῖτο τὰς διδασκαλίας, ἀλλ' οὐχ ὥσπερ σύνταξιν τῶν κυριακῶν ποιούμενος λογίων, ὥστε οὐδὲν ἥμαρτεν Μάρκος οὕτως ἔνια γράψας ὡς ἀπεμνημόνευσεν. ἑνὸς γὰρ ἐποιήσατο πρόνοιαν, τοῦ μηδὲν ὧν ἤκουσεν παραλιπεῖν ἢ ψεύσασθαί τι ἐν αὐτοῖς.

Papias, cf. Eusebius *H.E.* III.39.15.

Hieronymus

49

Marcus, discipulus et interpres Petri iuxta quod Petrum referentem audierat, rogatus Romae a fratribus breue scripsit euangelium. quod cum Petrus audisset, probauit et ecclesiis legendum sua auctoritate edidit, sicut scribit Clemens in sexto Ὑποτυπώσεων libro et Papias Hiera-

people there who had learned of Christ; that Bartholomew, one of the Apostles, had preached to them; and that he had left the writing of Matthew in Hebrew letters, which also was preserved to the time indicated.

B. F. Westcott, *A General Survey of the History of the Canon of the New Testament*, 7th ed. (London, 1896), pp. 83f.

JEROME

47

Matthew, who [is] also [called] Levi, [and who changed] from a publican to an Apostle, [was] the first one in Judea [to] "write" a Gospel of Christ in Hebrew letters and words for those from the circumcision who believed; [but] who translated it afterwards into Greek, is not sufficiently certain.

C. The Gospel of Mark

PAPIAS

48

And this the Presbyter used to say: Mark indeed, since he was the interpreter of Peter, wrote accurately, but not in order, the things either said or done by the Lord as much as he remembered. For he neither heard the Lord nor followed Him, but afterwards, as I have said, [heard and followed] Peter, who fitted his discourses to the needs [of his hearers] but not as if making a narrative of the Lord's sayings; consequently, Mark, writing some things just as he remembered, erred in nothing; for he was careful of one thing—not to omit anything of the things he had heard or to falsify anything in them.

JEROME

49

Mark, the disciple and interpreter of Peter, when asked by the brethren at Rome, wrote a short Gospel according to what he had heard Peter reporting. When Peter had heard of this, he approved it and authorized it[1] to be read in the churches, as Clement writes in the sixth book of the *Outlines* and [also]

[1] I.e. the Gospel.

politanus episcopus. meminit huius Marci et Petrus in prima epistula, sub nomine Babylonis figuraliter Romam significans Salutat uos quae est in Babylone coelecta et Marcus filius meus. adsumpto itaque euangelio quod ipse confecerat, perrexit Aegyptum et primus Alexandriae Christum adnuntians constituit ecclesiam tanta doctrina et uitae continentia, ut omnes sectatores Christi ad exemplum sui cogeret. denique Philon, disertissimus Iudaeorum, uidens Alexandriae primam ecclesiam adhuc iudaizantem quasi in laudem gentis suae librum super eorum conuersatione scripsit, et quomodo Lucas narrat Hierosolymae credentes omnia habuisse communia, sic ille quod Alexandriae sub Marco fieri doctore cernebat memoriae tradidit. mortuus est autem octauo Neronis anno et sepultus Alexandriae, succedente sibi Anniano.

Hieronymus *De uir. inl.* VIII, cf. Eusebius *H.E.* II.15.1-II.17.24.

Eusebius

50

Λουκᾶς δὲ τὸ μὲν γένος ὢν τῶν ἀπ' Ἀντιοχείας, τὴν ἐπιστήμην δὲ ἰατρός, τὰ πλεῖστα συγγεγονὼς τῷ Παύλῳ, καὶ τοῖς λοιποῖς δὲ οὐ παρέργως τῶν ἀποστόλων ὡμιληκώς, ἧς ἀπὸ τούτων προσεκτήσατο ψυχῶν θεραπευτικῆς ἐν δυσὶν ἡμῖν ὑποδείγματα θεοπνεύστοις κατέλιπεν βιβλίοις, τῷ τε εὐαγγελίῳ, ὃ καὶ χαράξαι μαρτύρεται καθ' ἃ παρέδοσαν αὐτῷ οἱ ἀπ' ἀρχῆς αὐτόπται καὶ ὑπηρέται γενόμενοι τοῦ λόγου, οἷς καί φησιν ἔτ' ἄνωθεν ἅπασι παρηκολουθηκέναι, καὶ ταῖς τῶν ἀποστόλων Πράξεσιν, ἃς οὐκέτι δι' ἀκοῆς, ὀφθαλμοῖς δὲ παραλαβὼν συνετάξατο· φασὶν δ' ὡς ἄρα τοῦ κατ' αὐτὸν εὐαγγελίου μνημονεύειν ὁ Παῦλος εἴωθεν, ὁπηνίκα ὡς περὶ ἰδίου τινὸς εὐαγγελίου γράφων ἔλεγεν κατὰ τὸ εὐαγγέλιόν μου.

Eusebius *H.E.* III.4.6.

Papias, the bishop of Hierapolis. Peter also mentions this Mark in his first Epistle, signifying Rome figuratively under the name of Babylon[1]: " The [church] which is in Babylon, elect together with you, and Mark, my son, salute you." And so, taking the Gospel which he had completed, he came to Egypt and, proclaiming Christ first in Alexandria, established the church in such doctrine and continence of life, that he induced all the followers of Christ [to follow] his example. Thereupon, Philo, the most learned of the Jews, noticing that the first church of Alexandria was still Jewish, wrote a book[2] concerning their manner of life, as it were in praise of his own people; and just as Luke narrates that the believers at Jerusalem had all things in common, so he[3] handed down to memory what he saw done under Mark, the teacher, at Alexandria. But he[4] died in the eighth year of Nero[5] and was buried at Alexandria, [and] Annianus succeeded him.

[1] I Pet. 5 : 13.
[2] *De vita contemplativa*—thought by many to be spurious, or if genuine, to describe not Christians but Jewish ascetics.
[3] I.e. Philo.   [4] I.e. Mark.   [5] A D. 62.

D. The Gospel of Luke

EUSEBIUS

50

Luke, in regard to race being of those of Antioch, but by profession a physician, since he had been very much with Paul and had no mean association with the rest of the Apostles, left us examples of the therapy of souls, which he acquired from them, in two inspired books: the Gospel which he testifies that he also wrote according to what those handed down to him who were eyewitnesses from the beginning and ministers of the word, all of whom he also says he had followed even from the beginning; and the Acts of the Apostles which he composed from what he had learned, not by hearing but with [his] eyes. But men say that Paul was accustomed to refer to his Gospel whenever, writing as it were about some Gospel of his own, he said, " according to my Gospel."

Hieronymus

51

Lucas, medicus Antiochensis, ut eius scripta indicant, Graeci sermonis non ignarus fuit, sectator apostoli Pauli et omnis eius peregrinationis comes, scripsit euangelium, de quo idem Paulus Misimus, inquit, cum illo fratrem cuius laus est in euangelio per omnes ecclesias, et ad Colossenses Salutat uos Lucas medicus carissimus, et ad Timotheum, Lucas est mecum solus. aliud quoque edidit uolumen egregium quod titulo Apostolicorum πράξεων praenotatur, cuius historia usque ad biennium Romae commorantis Pauli peruenit, id est ad quartum Neronis annum. ex quo intelligimus in eadem urbe librum esse conpositum. igitur περιόδους Pauli et Theclae et totam baptizati leonis fabulam inter apocryphas scripturas conputemus. quale enim est, ut indiuiduus comes apostoli inter ceteras eius res hoc solum ignoraverit? sed et Tertullianus, uicinus illorum temporum, refert presbyterum quendam in Asia, σπουδαστήν apostoli Pauli, conuictum apud Iohannem quod auctor esset libri, et confessum se hoc Pauli amore fecisse, loco excidisse. quidam suspicantur, quotiescumque Paulus in epistulis suis dicat Iuxta euangelium meum, de Lucae significare uolumine et Lucam non solum ab apostolo Paulo didicisse euangelium qui cum Domino in carne non fuerat, sed et a ceteris apostolis. quod ipse quoque in principio uoluminis sui declarat dicens Sicut tradiderunt nobis qui a principio ipsi uiderunt et ministri fuerunt sermonis. igitur euangelium, sicut audierat scripsit; Acta uero apostolorum, sicut uiderat ipse, conposuit. sepultus est Constantinopolim, ad quam urbem, uicesimo Constantii anno, ossa eius, cum reliquiis Andreae apostoli, translata sunt.

Hieronymus *De uir. inl.* VII.

JEROME

51

Luke, a physician of Antioch, was not ignorant of the Greek language, as his writings indicate; a follower of the Apostle Paul and a companion of all his journeying, he wrote the Gospel concerning which Paul also says: " We have sent together with him the brother[1] whose praise is in the Gospel throughout all the churches;[2] and to the Colossians [he wrote]: " Luke the most beloved physician salutes you,"[3] and to Timothy: " Only Luke is with me."[4] He published also another excellent book entitled The Acts of the Apostles whose narrative goes up to Paul's stay of two years in Rome, that is to the fourth year of Nero.[5] From this we understand that the book was composed in the same city. Therefore, let us reckon among the Apocryphal writings *The Acts*[6] *of Paul and Thecla* and the entire fable about the baptized lion. For how could it be[7] that an inseparable companion of the Apostle, among other things concerning him, would have been ignorant of this [incident] only? But even Tertullian, [who lived] near those times, reports that a certain presbyter in Asia, an admirer of the Apostle Paul, when he had been convicted before John of being the author of the book, and had confessed that he had written it out of regard for Paul, fell from his position. Some suppose that, whenever, Paul says in his Epistles, " according to my Gospel," he is referring to the book of Luke, and that Luke learned the Gospel not only from the Apostle Paul who had not been with the Lord in the flesh, but also from other Apostles. " This " he himself also declares in the beginning of his book, saying:[8] "As they delivered [them][9] to us who from the beginning were eyewitnesses and ministers of the word." Therefore, he wrote the Gospel just as he had heard; but the Acts of the Apostles he composed just as he himself had seen. He is buried in Constantinople, to which city, in the twentieth year of Constantius,[10] his bones, together with the remains of the Apostle Andrew, were transferred.

---

[1] I.e. Titus. [2] II Cor. 8 : 18. [3] Col. 4 : 14. [4] II Tim. 4 : 11.
[5] A. D. 58. [6] Literally " Journeyings." [7] Literally " What kind of a thing is it."
[8] Lk. 1 : 2. [9] I.e. " the things which have been accomplished among us," Luke 1 : 1.
[10] A. D. 357.

Theophilus

52

Ὁπότε δὲ ἠθέλησεν ὁ θεὸς ποιῆσαι ὅσα ἐβουλεύσατο, τοῦτον τὸν λόγον ἐγέννησεν προφορικόν, πρωτότοκον πάσης κτίσεως, οὐ κενωθεὶς αὐτὸς τοῦ λόγου, ἀλλὰ λόγον γεννήσας καὶ τῷ λόγῳ αὐτοῦ διὰ παντὸς ὁμιλῶν. ὅθεν διδάσκουσιν ἡμᾶς αἱ ἅγιαι γραφαὶ καὶ πάντες οἱ πνευματοφόροι, ἐξ ὧν Ἰωάννης λέγει Ἐν ἀρχῇ ἦν ὁ λόγος, καὶ λόγος ἦν πρὸς τὸν θεόν· δεικνὺς ὅτι ἐν πρώτοις μόνος ἦν ὁ θεὸς καὶ ἐν αὐτῷ ὁ λόγος. ἔπειτα λέγει Καὶ θεὸς ἦν ὁ λόγος· πάντα δι' αὐτοῦ ἐγένετο καὶ χωρὶς αὐτοῦ ἐγένετο οὐδὲ ἕν. θεὸς οὖν ὢν ὁ λόγος καὶ ἐκ θεοῦ πεφυκώς, ὁπόταν βούληται ὁ πατὴρ τῶν ὅλων πέμπει αὐτὸν εἴς τινα τόπον, ὃς παραγινόμενος καὶ ἀκούεται καὶ ὁρᾶται, πεμπόμενος ὑπ' αὐτοῦ, καὶ ἐν τόπῳ εὑρίσκεται.

Theophilus *Ad Autolycum* II.22.

Irenaeus

53

Hanc fidem annuntians Iohannes Domini discipulus, uolens per euangelii annuntiationem auferre eum, qui a Cerintho inseminatus erat hominibus errorem, et multo prius ab his qui dicuntur Nicolaitae, qui sunt uulsio eius quae falso cognominatur scientiae, ut confunderet eos, et suaderet quoniam unus deus qui omnia fecit per verbum suum; et non, quemadmodum illi dicunt, alterum quidem fabricatorem, alium autem patrem Domini: et alium quidem fabricatoris filium, alterum uero de superioribus Christum, quem et impassibilem perseverasse, descendentem in Iesum filium fabricatoris, et iterum reuolasse in suum pleroma: et initium quidem esse monogenem; Logon autem verum filium unigeniti; et eam conditionem quae est secundum nos, non a primo Deo factam, sed a virtute aliqua valde deorsum subiecta, et abscissa ab eorum communicatione quae sunt inuisibilia et innominabilia . . . . sic inchoavit in ea quae est secundum euuangelium doctrina: in principio erat uerbum . . . .

Irenaeus, *Adu. haer.* III.11.7.

E. The Gospel of John

THEOPHILUS (c. A. D. 170-180)

52

But when God determined to do the things which He had purposed, He brought forth this utterable Word, the first-born of all creation; He himself was not emptied of the Word but bringing forth [the] Word He always had consort with His Word. Hence the Holy Scriptures and all the inspired [writers] teach us [as] one of these, John, says: "In the beginning was the Word, and [the] Word was with God;" showing that at the first God was alone and the Word was in Him. Then he says: "And the Word was God; all things were made by Him and without Him not a thing was made." Therefore, the Word, being God and proceeding by nature from God, whenever the Father of the universe determines, He sends Him to a certain place; coming He is both heard and seen; being sent by Him, He is also found in [that] place.

IRENAEUS

53

John, the Lord's disciple, proclaims this faith [and] desires, by the proclamation of the Gospel, to remove that error which had been disseminated among men by Cerinthus and much earlier by those who are called Nicolaitans who are an offshoot of that knowledge falsely so called, that he might confound them and persuade [them] that there [is] one God who made all things through His Word, and not as they say that the Creator was surely one, and the Father of the Lord another; and that the Son of the Creator was surely one, but the Christ from higher spheres another, [and] that He lived impassible to the end, descended on Jesus the Son of the Creator, and returned again to His Pleroma; and that the Only-begotten was indeed the beginning, but that the Word was the true Son of the Only-begotten; and that the world in which we "live" has not been made by the Supreme God, but by some power lying far below Him and excluded from communion with things invisible and ineffable.... Thus he began "with" the teaching [of] the Gospel: "In the beginning was the Word...."

Hieronymus

54

Iohannes apostolus quem Iesus amauit plurimum, filius Zebedaei et frater Iacobi apostoli quem Herodes post passionem Domini decollauit, nouissimus omnium scripsit euangelium, rogatus ab Asiae episcopis, aduersus Cerinthum aliosque haereticos et maxime tunc Ebionitarum dogma consurgens, qui adserunt Christum ante Mariam non fuisse. unde etiam compulsus est diuinam eius natiuitatem edicere. sed et aliam causam huius scripturae ferunt, quod, cum legisset Matthaei, Marci et Lucae uolumina, probauerit quidem textum historiae et uera eos dixisse firmauerit, sed unius tantum anni in quo et passus est post carcerem Iohannis, historiam texuisse. praetermisso itaque anno cuius acta a tribus exposita fuerant, superioris temporis, antequam Iohannes clauderetur in carcerem, gesta narrauit, sicut manifestum esse poterit his qui diligenter quattuor euangeliorum uolumina legerint. quae res et διαφωνίαν quae uidetur Iohannis esse cum ceteris, tollit.

Scripsit autem et unam epistulam cuius exordium est Quod fuit ab initio, quod audiuimus et uidimus oculis nostris, quod perspeximus et manus nostrae temptauerunt de uerbo uitae, quae ab uniuersis ecclesiasticis et eruditis uiris probatur. reliquae autem duae quarum principium est Senior electae dominae et natis eius et sequentis, Senior Gaio carissimo, quem ego diligo in ueritate Iohannis presbyteri adseruntur, cuius et hodie alterum sepulcrum apud Ephesum ostenditur; et nonnulli putant duas memorias eiusdem Iohannis euangelistae esse; super qua re, cum per ordinem ad Papiam auditorem eius uentum fuerit, disseremus.

Quarto decimo igitur anno, secundam post Neronem persecutionem mouente Domitiano, in Patmos insulam relegatus, scripsit Apocalypsin, quam interpretantur Iustinus martyr et Irenaeus. Interfecto autem Domitiano et actis eius ob nimiam crudelitatem a senatu rescissis, sub Nerua redit Ephesum ibique usque ad Traianum principem perseuerans totas Asiae fundauit rexitque ecclesias et confectus senio et sexagesimo octauo post passionem Domini anno mortuus, iuxta eandem urbem sepultus est.

Hieronymus *De uir. inl.* IX.

---

[1]Herod Agrippa I.   [2]A. D. 44.   [3]I Jn. 1 : 1.   [4]II Jn. 1.
[5]III Jn 1.   [6]I.e. of Jn.   [7]A. D. 95.   [8]A. D. 98–117.
[9]That is A. D. 99–100 as Jerome in his Latin version of Eusebius dates the passion in the eighteenth year of Tiberius A. D. 31–32.

The Gospel of John

JEROME

54

a John, the Apostle whom Jesus loved very much, the son of Zebedee and the brother of James whom Herod[1] beheaded[2] after the passion of the Lord, last of all, when asked by the bishops of Asia, wrote a Gospel against Cerinthus and other heretics and especially [against] the dogma of the Ebionites which sprang up at that time, who assert that Christ did not exist before Mary. Wherefore also he was compelled to establish his divine nativity. But they report another cause of this writing, that, when he had read the books of Matthew, Mark, and Luke, he definitely approved of the "verity" of the narrative and affirmed that they had reported real [facts], but [he said] that they had told the history of only the one year after the imprisonment of John, in which [the Lord] also suffered. Therefore, omitting this year whose events had been set forth by [these] three, he narrated the deeds of an earlier time before John was shut up in prison, as will be manifest to those who would diligently read the books of the four Gospels. This removes also the disagreement which seems to exist between John and the others.

b But he wrote also one Epistle whose beginning is[3]: "That which was from the beginning, which we have heard and have seen with our eyes, which we beheld and our hands have handled concerning the word of life." It is accepted by all ecclesiastical and learned men. But the other two, the beginning [of the first] of which is:[4] "The elder to the elect lady and her children," and the "other one"[5] [whose beginning is]: "The elder to Gaius, the most beloved, whom I love in truth," they say are of John the Presbyter, whose sepulchre is shown even today at Ephesus [to be] one of two; and some think that both "gravestones" are of one and the same John the Evangelist. We shall speak about this matter in due course when we come to Papias, his hearer.[6]

Therefore, in the fourteenth year [of his reign],[7] when Domitian began the second persecution after Nero, when he had been banished to the island of Patmos, he wrote the Apocalypse, which Justin Martyr and Irenaeus interpret[ed]. But when Domitian had been killed and his decree rescinded by the Senate because of excessive cruelty, he returned to Ephesus under Nerva and, continuing there even until [the time of] the Emperor Trajan,[8] he established and directed all the churches of Asia, and, weakened with age he died in the sixty-eighth [year] after the passion of the Lord.[9] He was buried near the same city.

Fragmentum euangelii secundum Iohannem

55

Οἱ ἰουδαιοι ημε[ιν ομκ εξεστιν αποκτειναι]
ουδενα ϊνα ο λο[γος του ιησου πληρωθη ον ει]
πεν σημαινω[ν ποιω θανατω ημελλεν απο]
θνησκειν ισ[ηλθεν ουν παλιν εις το πραιτω]
ριον ο π[ιλατος και εφωνησεν τον ιησουν]
και ειπ[εν αυτω συ ει ο βασιλευς των ιου]
[δ]αιω[ν απεκριθη ιησους κτλ.

. . . .

[εγω εις το]υτο γ[ε]γεννημαι
[και εις τουτο εληλυθα εις τον κο]σμον ϊνα μαρτυ
[ρησω τη αληθεια πας ο ων] εκ της αληθε[ι]
[ας ακουει μου της φωνης] λεγει αυτω
[ο πιλατος τι εστιν αληθεια κ]αι τουτο
[ειπων παλιν εξηλθεν προς] τους ιο[υ]
[δαιους και λεγει αυτοις εγω ουδ]εμι[αν]

C. H. Roberts, *Catalogue of the Greek and Latin Papyri in the John Rylands Library, Manchester* (London, 1938), p. 2.

Irenaeus

56

Quoniam autem is Lucas inseparabilis fuit a Paulo, et cooperarius eius in euangelio, ipse facit manifestum, non glorians, sed ab ipsa productus ueritate. separatis enim, inquit, a Paulo, et Barnaba et Iohanne, qui uocabatur Marcus, et cum nauigassent Cyprum Nos uenimus in Troadem : et cum uidisset Paulus per somnium uirum Macedonem, dicentem Ueniens in Macedoniam opitulare nobis Paule; statim, ait, quaesiuimus proficisci in Macedoniam, intelligentes quoniam prouocauit nos Dominus euangelizare eis.

Irenaeus *Adu. haer.* III.14.1.

FRAGMENT FROM THE JOHN RYLANDS LIBRARY (c. A. D. 100-150)
(John 18 : 31-34, 37-38)

55

*That the w*or*d* of Jesus might be fulfilled, which He sp*oke showing* by what death He wa*s to die, the Jews* [said to Him]: "It is not lawful for us to put *anyone* to death." *P*ilate, therefore, entered again into the praeto*rium* and called Jesus and said to Him: "Are you the King of the J*ews?*" Jesus answered, etc.

". . . for t*his was I born* and for this have I come into the wo*rld that* I may *bear witness* to the truth. Every one who is *of the tr*uth hears my voice." Pilate *said to Him*: "What is truth?" A*nd* saying *this*, he went out again to *the Jews* and said to them: "I [find] *no* . . . ."

C. H. Roberts, *An Unpublished Fragment of the Fourth Gospel in the John Rylands Library* (Manchester, 1935).

F. The Acts of the Apostles

IRENAEUS

56

Now, that this Luke, was inseparable from Paul, and his fellow-worker in the Gospel, he himself made clear, not vaunting, but guided by truth itself. For when both Barnabas and John, who was called Mark, had departed from Paul and had sailed to Cyprus,[1] he says: "We arrived at Troas." And when Paul had seen a Macedonian man in a dream saying: "Come over into Macedonia and help us, Paul," he says: "Immediately we sought to proceed into Macedonia, knowing that the Lord had called us to proclaim the Gospel to them."[2]

[1] Acts 15 : 39.   [2] Cf. Acts 16 : 9f.

Clemens Alexandrinus

57

. . . . . καθὸ καὶ ὁ Λουκᾶς ἐν ταῖς Πράξεσι τῶν ἀποστόλων ἀπομνημονεύει τὸν Παῦλον λέγοντα "Ἄνδρες Ἀθηναῖοι, κατὰ πάντα ὡς δεισιδαιμονεστέρους ὑμᾶς θεωρῶ.

Clemens Alexandrinus *Stromata* V.82.4.

Marcionis Prologi

58

Romani sunt in partibus Italiae. hi praeuenti sunt a falsis apostolis et sub nomine domini nostri Iesu Christi in legem et prophetas erant inducti. hos reuocat apostolus ad ueram euangelicam fidem scribens eis a Corintho.

59

Corinthii sunt Achaei. et hi similiter ab apostolis audierunt uerbum ueritatis et subuersi multifarie a falsis apostolis, quidam a philosophiae uerbosa eloquentia, alii a secta legis Iudiciae inducti. hos reuocat ad ueram et euangelicam sapientiam scribens eis ab Epheso per Timotheum.

60

Post actam paenitentiam consolatorias scribit eis a Troade et conlaudans eos hortatur ad meliora.

CLEMENT OF ALEXANDRIA

57

... even as Luke, in the Acts of the Apostles, makes mention of Paul, who said: " O, men of Athens, in all things I perceive that you are very religious."[1]

[1] Acts 17 : 22.

G. Paul's Epistles

MARCIONITE PROLOGUES
ROMANS

58

The Romans " live " in the regions of Italy. They had been reached beforehand by false apostles, and under the name of our Lord Jesus Christ they were misled into the Law and the Prophets. The Apostle, writing to them from Corinth, calls them back to the true evangelical faith.

I CORINTHIANS

59

The Corinthians are Achaeans. And they similarly heard the word of truth from the Apostles, but they were subverted in many ways by false apostles—some were misled by verbose eloquence of philosophy, others by a sect of the Jewish law. [Paul], writing to them from Ephesus by Timothy, calls them back to the truth and evangelical wisdom.

II CORINTHIANS

60

After [their] penitence, he writes a consoling [letter] to them from Troas and praising them, he exhorts them unto better things.

61

Galatae sunt Graeci. hi uerbum ueritatis primum ab apostolo acceperunt, sed post discessum eius temptati sunt a falsis apostolis, ut in legem et circumcisionem uerterentur. hos apostolus reuocat ad fidem ueritatis scribens eis ab Epheso.

62

Ephesii sunt Asiani. hi accepto uerbo ueritatis persteterunt in fide. hos conlaudat apostolus scribens eis ab urbe Roma de carcere per Tychicum diaconum.

63

Philippenses sunt Machedones. hi accepto uerbo ueritatis persteterunt in fide nec receperunt falsos apostolos. hos apostolus conlaudat scribens eis a Roma de carcere per Epaphroditum.

64

Colossenses et hi sicut Laudicenses sunt Asiani. et ipsi praeuenti erant a pseudoapostolis nec ad hos accessit ipse apostolus, sed et hos per epistulam recorrigit. audierant enim uerbum ab Archippo qui et ministerium in eos accepit. ergo apostolus iam ligatus scribit eis ab Epheso.

65

Thessalonicenses sunt Machedones in Christo Iesu, qui accepto uerbo ueritatis persteterunt in fide etiam in persecutione ciuium suorum, praeterea nec receperunt ea quae a falsis apostolis dicebantur. hos conlaudat apostolus scribens eis ab Athenis.

GALATIANS

61

The Galatians are Greeks. They received the word of truth first from the Apostle, but after his departure they were tempted by false apostles that they might be converted to the law and circumcision. The Apostle calls them back to the true faith [by] writing to them from Ephesus.

EPHESIANS

62

The Ephesians are Asians. After [they] had accepted the truth, they persevered in faith. The Apostle praises them, writing to them from the city of Rome, from the prison, by Tychicus the deacon.

PHILIPPIANS

63

The Philippians are Macedonians. They persevered in faith after [they] had accepted the word of truth and they did not receive false apostles. The Apostle praises them, writing to them from Rome from the prison, by Epaphroditus.

COLOSSIANS

64

The Colossians, they also, just as the Laodiceans, are Asians. They themselves had been reached beforehand by false apostles. The Apostle himself did not come to them, but he corrects even them by an epistle. For they had heard the word from Archippus who received the ministry to them. The Apostle then, after he had already been arrested, writes to them from Ephesus.

I THESSALONIANS

65

The Thessalonians are Macedonians in Christ Jesus, who after [they] had accepted the word of truth, persevered in faith even during the persecution "by" their [fellow]-citizens; and furthermore they did not accept those things which were advocated by false apostles. The Apostle praises them when he writes to them from Athens.

66

Ad Thessalonicenses secundam scribit et notum facit eis de temporibus nouissimis et de aduersarii detectione. scribit ab Athenis.

67

Timotheum instruit et docet de ordinatione episcopatus et diaconii et omnis ecclesiasticae disciplinae.

68

Item Timotheo scribit de exhortatione martyrii et omnis regulae ueritatis et quid futurum sit temporibus nouissimis et de sua passione.

69

Titum commonefacit et instruit de constitutione presbyterii et de spiritali conuersatione et hereticis uitandis qui in scripturis Iudaicis credunt.

70

Philemoni familiares litteras facit pro Onesimo seruo eius. scribit autem ei a Roma de carcere.

Erwin Preuschen, *Analecta* (*Sammlung ausgewählter kirchen- und dogmengeschichtlicher Quellenschriften*, Achtes Heft, Zweiter Teil), pp. 85–88.

II THESSALONIANS

66

He writes a second [epistle] to the Thessalonians and makes known to them both [things] about the last times and about the exposing of the Adversary. He writes from Athens.

I TIMOTHY

67

He instructs and teaches Timothy concerning ordination to the episcopate and to the diaconate and of the whole ecclesiastical order.

II TIMOTHY

68

He writes again to Timothy about the exhortation to martyrdom and of the entire rule of faith; also what would be in the last times and about his suffering.

TITUS

69

He reminds and instructs Titus concerning the constitution of a presbytery and concerning spiritual walk and heretics who believe in Jewish books, and who must be avoided.

PHILEMON

70

He writes a personal letter to Philemon on behalf of his slave Onesimus. He, however,[1] writes to him from Rome from the prison.

---

[1] To contrast Paul, a free man in prison, with Onesimus, a slave in liberty.
Dom de Bruyne, " Prologues bibliques d'origine Marcionite, " *Rev. Bénéd.*, 24 (1907), pp. 1–16; P. Corssen, " Zur Überlieferungsgeschichte des Römerbriefs," *ZNTW.*, Vol. 10 (1909), pp. 1–45, 97–103; W. Mundle, " Der Herkunft der ' marcionitischen ' Prologe zu den Paulinischen Briefen," *ZNTW.*, Vol. 24 (1925), pp. 56–77; Adolf v. Harnack, " Der marcionitische Ursprung der ältesten Vulgata-Prologe zu den Paulusbriefen," *ZNTW.*, Vol. 24 (1925), pp. 204–218; M.-J. La Grange, " Les Prologues prétendus Marcionites," *Revue Biblique*, Vol. 35 (1926), pp. 161–173.

Clemens Alexandrinus

71

Κέχρηται δ' ἐν αὐτοῖς καὶ ταῖς ἀπὸ τῶν ἀντιλεγομένων γραφῶν μαρτυρίαις, τῆς τε λεγομένης Σολομῶνος Σοφίας καὶ τῆς Ἰησοῦ τοῦ Σιρὰχ καὶ τῆς πρὸς Ἑβραίους ἐπιστολῆς τῆς τε Βαρναβᾶ καὶ Κλήμεντος καὶ Ἰούδα . . . .

Clemens, cf. Eusebius H.E. VI.13.6.

72

Καὶ τὴν πρὸς Ἑβραίους δὲ ἐπιστολὴν Παύλου μὲν εἶναί φησιν, γεγράφθαι δὲ Ἑβραίοις Ἑβραϊκῇ φωνῇ, Λουκᾶν δὲ φιλοτίμως αὐτὴν μεθερμηνεύσαντα ἐκδοῦναι τοῖς Ἕλλησιν, ὅθεν τὸν αὐτὸν χρῶτα εὑρίσκεσθαι κατὰ τὴν ἑρμηνείαν ταύτης τε τῆς ἐπιστολῆς καὶ τῶν Πράξεων· μὴ προγεγράφθαι δὲ τὸ Παῦλος ἀπόστολος εἰκότως· Ἑβραίοις γάρ, φησίν, ἐπιστέλλων πρόληψιν εἰληφόσιν κατ' αὐτοῦ καὶ ὑποπτεύουσιν αὐτόν, συνετῶς πάνυ οὐκ ἐν ἀρχῇ ἀπέτρεψεν αὐτούς, τὸ ὄνομα θείς. εἶτα ὑποβὰς ἐπιλέγει "Ἤδη δέ, ὡς ὁ μακάριος ἔλεγεν πρεσβύτερος, ἐπεὶ ὁ κύριος, ἀπόστολος ὢν τοῦ παντοκράτορος, ἀπεστάλη πρὸς Ἑβραίους, διὰ μετριότητα ὁ Παῦλος, ὡς ἂν εἰς τὰ ἔθνη ἀπεσταλμένος, οὐκ ἐγγράφει ἑαυτὸν Ἑβραίων ἀπόστολον διά τε τὴν πρὸς τὸν κύριον τιμὴν διά τε τὸ ἐκ περιουσίας καὶ τοῖς Ἑβραίοις ἐπιστέλλειν, ἐθνῶν κήρυκα ὄντα καὶ ἀπόστολον.

Clemens, cf. Eusebius H.E. VI.14.2–4.

Origen

73

Ἔτι πρὸς τούτοις περὶ τῆς Πρὸς Ἑβραίους ἐπιστολῆς ἐν ταῖς εἰς αὐτὴν Ὁμιλίαις ταῦτα διαλαμβάνει· ὅτι ὁ χαρακτὴρ τῆς λέξεως τῆς Πρὸς Ἑβραίους ἐπιγεγραμμένης ἐπιστολῆς οὐκ ἔχει τὸ ἐν λόγῳ ἰδιωτικὸν τοῦ ἀποστόλου, ὁμολογήσαντος ἑαυτὸν ἰδιώτην εἶναι τῷ λόγῳ, τοῦτ' ἐστιν τῇ φράσει, ἀλλ' ἐστὶν ἡ ἐπιστολὴ συνθέσει τῆς λέξεως Ἑλληνικωτέρα, πᾶς ὁ ἐπιστάμενος κρίνειν

H. Hebrews

CLEMENT OF ALEXANDRIA

71

But in them (the *Miscellanies*) he made use even of the testimonies of the disputed writings, both the so-called Wisdom of Solomon, and [the Wisdom] of Jesus the son of Sirach, and the Epistle to the Hebrews, and [the Epistles] of Barnabas and Clement and Jude . . . .

72

He says that the Epistle to the Hebrews is also of Paul, but that it was written for the Hebrews in the Hebrew tongue, but that Luke translated it carefully [and] published it for the Greeks; hence [he says], due to the translation, the same style is found both [in] the Epistle and [in] the Acts. But [he adds] that [the words] "The Apostle Paul," were naturally not prefixed. For he says: "In writing to the Hebrews, who were prejudiced against him and suspicious of him, he, very wisely, did not repel them right away, by putting his name." Then proceeding he adds: "But now, as the blessed elder used to say, since the Lord, being the apostle of the Almighty, was sent to the Hebrews, Paul, due to modesty, since he had been sent to the Gentiles, does not style himself as the apostle of the Hebrews, both by reason of his reverence for the Lord, and for the sake of writing also to the Hebrews out of [his] abundance, although he was the herald and apostle of the Gentiles."

ORIGEN

73

Further, in addition to these, he discusses the following separately about the Epistle to the Hebrews in his *Homilies* on it: "That the character of the diction of the epistle, entitled 'To the Hebrews,' does not have the individual [touch] of the Apostle in speech, who confessed that he is rude in speech,[1] that is in expression, but that the epistle is more Greek-like in the composition of [its] diction, everyone would agree who understands

[1] II Cor. 11 : 6.

φράσεων διαφορὰς ὁμολογῆσαι ἄν. πάλιν τε αὖ ὅτι τὰ νοήματα τῆς ἐπιστολῆς θαυμάσιά ἐστιν καὶ οὐ δεύτερα τῶν ἀποστολικῶν ὁμολογουμένων γραμμάτων, καὶ τοῦτο ἂν συμφῆσαι εἶναι ἀληθὲς πᾶς ὁ προσέχων τῇ ἀναγνώσει τῇ ἀποστολικῇ.

Τούτοις μεθ' ἕτερα ἐπιφέρει λέγων· "Ἐγὼ δὲ ἀποφαινόμενος εἴποιμ' ἂν ὅτι τὰ μὲν νοήματα τοῦ ἀποστόλου ἐστίν, ἡ δὲ φράσις καὶ ἡ σύνθεσις ἀπομνημονεύσαντός τινος τὰ ἀποστολικὰ καὶ ὥσπερ σχολιογραφήσαντός τινος τὰ εἰρημένα ὑπὸ τοῦ διδασκάλου. εἴ τις οὖν ἐκκλησία ἔχει ταύτην τὴν ἐπιστολὴν ὡς Παύλου, αὕτη εὐδοκιμείτω καὶ ἐπὶ τούτῳ· οὐ γὰρ εἰκῇ οἱ ἀρχαῖοι ἄνδρες ὡς Παύλου αὐτὴν παραδεδώκασιν. τίς δὲ ὁ γράψας τὴν ἐπιστολήν, τὸ μὲν ἀληθὲς θεὸς οἶδεν, ἡ δὲ εἰς ἡμᾶς φθάσασα ἱστορία ὑπὸ τινῶν μὲν λεγόντων ὅτι Κλήμης, ὁ γενόμενος ἐπίσκοπος Ῥωμαίων, ἔγραψεν τὴν ἐπιστολήν, ὑπὸ τινῶν δὲ ὅτι Λουκᾶς, ὁ γράψας τὸ εὐαγγέλιον καὶ τὰς Πράξεις.

Origen, cf. Eusebius *H.E.* VI.25.11-14.

Tertullianus

74

Uolo tamen ex redundantia alicuius etiam comitis apostolorum testimonium superducere, idoneum confirmandi de proximo iure disciplinam magistrorum. extat enim et Barnabae titulus ad Hebraeos, a deo satis auctorati uiri, ut quem Paulus iuxta se constituerit in abstinentiae tenore Aut ego solus et Barnabas non habemus operandi potestatem? et utique receptior apud ecclesias epistola Barnabae illo apocrypho Pastore moechorum. monens itaque discipulos omissis omnibus initiis ad perfectionem magis tendere nec rursus fundamenta paenitentiae iacere ab operibus mortuorum, Impossibile est enim, inquit, eos, qui semel inluminati sunt et donum caeleste gustauerunt, et participauerunt spiritum sanctum et uerbum dei dulce gustauerunt, occidente iam aeuo cum exciderint, rursus reuocari in paenitentiam, refigentes cruci in semetipsos filium dei et dedecorantes.

Tertullianus *De pudicitia* XX.

[how] to judge differences of style. Over and again [he says] that the thoughts of the epistle are excellent and not second to the acknowledged apostolic writings; everyone, who gives attention to the reading of the Apostle, would agree that this also is true."

Furthermore, he adds to this, saying: " But as it seems to me, I would say, that the thoughts are of the Apostle but the expression and composition are of one who recalled the "Apostle's" [teachings], and who had made " exact " notes of the things said by [his] teacher. If some church, then, regards this letter as of Paul, let it be content with this [view]. For not without reason did the men of old hand it down as of Paul. But who wrote the letter, God really knows. However, the account, which came to us, as contended by some, is that Clement, who became bishop of the Romans, wrote the epistle, but [it is contended] by others that Luke, who wrote the Gospel and the Acts, did.

TERTULLIAN

74

I wish, however, to superadd redundantly also the testimony of a certain comrade of the Apostles, fit to confirm most rightly the discipline of the masters. For there is extant with the title " To the Hebrews " an [epistle] of Barnabas, a man sufficiently authorized by God, whom Paul placed on a par with himself in observance of abstinence [saying]: " Or I alone and Barnabas have not we the power of working? "[1] And certainly, the *Epistle of Barnabas* is more generally received among the churches than that apocryphal *Shepherd* of the adulterers. And warning the disciples accordingly rather to strive after perfection and not to lay again the foundations of repentance by works of defunct things, since all the rites[2] have been abandoned, he says: " For, it is impossible that those who have once been illuminated, and have tasted the heavenly sacrifice, and have participated in the Holy Spirit, and have tasted the sweet word of God, when they have fallen away—their life already declining—[could] be called unto repentance again, crucifying again in themselves the Son of God, and dishonoring Him."[3]

[1] I Cor. 9 : 6.   [2] Of the Jewish law.   [3] Hebr. 6 : 4–6.

Clemens Alexandrinus

75

Ἐν δὲ ταῖς Ὑποτυπώσεσιν ξυνελόντα εἰπεῖν πάσης τῆς ἐνδιαθήκου γραφῆς ἐπιτετμημένας πεποίηται διηγήσεις, μηδὲ τὰς ἀντιλεγομένας παρελθών, τὴν Ἰούδα λέγω καὶ τὰς λοιπὰς καθολικὰς ἐπιστολὰς τήν τε Βαρναβᾶ, καὶ τὴν Πέτρου λεγομένην Ἀποκάλυψιν.

Clemens, cf. Eusebius H.E. VI.14.1.

Prologus

76

Canones noui testamenti primus Petrus scripsit, secundus Iacobus, tertius Matheus, quartus Iudas, quintus Paulus, sextus Barnabas, septimus Lucas, octauus Marcus, nonus Iohannes. quare primus Iacobus in ordine epistularum ponitur, cum primus Petrus in ordine canonis, scripsit? hac de causa fuit prerogatiua apostolici ordinis, ut quidam interpretantur [significat] uel prestantius est, ut adfirmant alii, ut Petrus ponatur primus, cum primus scripsit. dicunt quidam epistula Iacobi quod ab illo sit edita eius nomine, quorum opinio falsa est.

Erwin Preuschen, op. cit., p. 93.

Iustinus Martyr

77

Καὶ ἐπειδὴ καὶ παρ' ἡμῖν ἀνήρ τις, ᾧ ὄνομα Ἰωάννης, εἷς τῶν ἀποστόλων τοῦ Χριστοῦ, ἐν ἀποκαλύψει γενομένῃ αὐτῷ χίλια ἔτη ποιήσειν ἐν Ἱερουσαλὴμ τοὺς τῷ ἡμετέρῳ Χριστῷ πιστεύσαντας προεφήτευσε καὶ μετὰ ταῦτα τὴν καθολικὴν καί, συνελόντι φάναι, αἰωνίαν ὁμοθυμαδὸν ἅμα πάντων ἀνάστασιν γενήσεσθαι καὶ κρίσιν.

Iustinus Dialogus LXXXI.4.

I. The Catholic Epistles

CLEMENT OF ALEXANDRIA

75

But in his *Outlines*, to speak briefly, he presented condensed discussions of all the "canonical" books, without omitting the disputed ones—I mean Jude and the other Catholic Epistles, and *Barnabas* and the so-called *Apocalypse of Peter*.

PROLOGUE TO THE CATHOLIC EPISTLES

76

Canons of the New Testament [are]: Peter wrote first, second James, third Matthew, fourth Jude, fifth Paul, sixth Barnabas, seventh Luke, eighth Mark, ninth John. For what reason is James placed first in the order of the epistles, whereas Peter wrote first in the order of the canon? It was by virtue of the prerogative of apostolic order, as some interpret it [×it signifies×], or it is, as others affirm, because of [his historical] priority that Peter should be placed first, since he wrote first. Some say that the Epistle of James was edited under his name by him,[1] [but] their opinion is false.

[1] I.e. Peter.
Donadt de Bruyne, "Un prologue inconnu des épitres catholiques," *Reveu Bénéd.*, 23 (1906), pp. 82–87.

J. The Apocalypse

JUSTIN MARTYR (c. A. D. 147–161)

77

And further, there was a certain man, even with us, whose name was John, one of the Apostles of Christ, who prophesied in a revelation which came to him that those who believed in our Christ will spend a thousand years in Jerusalem, and after that, the general and, in short, the eternal resurrection and judgment of all will come to pass at one and the same time.

Hippolytus

78

Ταῦτα μὲν οὖν προφητεύει Ἡσαΐας· ἴδωμεν δὲ εἰ τὰ ὅμοια αὐτῷ ἐφθέγξατο Ἰωάννης. οὗτος γὰρ ἐν Πάτμῳ τῇ νήσῳ ὢν ὁρᾷ ἀποκάλυψιν μυστηρίων φρικτῶν, ἅτινα διηγούμενος ἀφθόνως καὶ ἑτέρους διδάσκει. λέγε μοι, ὦ μακάριε Ἰωάννη, ἀπόστολε καὶ μαθητὰ τοῦ κυρίου, τί εἶδες καὶ τί ἤκουσας περὶ Βαβυλῶνος. γρηγόρησον καὶ εἰπέ· καὶ γὰρ αὐτή σε ἐξώρισεν. καὶ ἦλθεν εἷς τῶν ἑπτὰ ἀγγέλων τῶν ἐχόντων τὰς ἑπτὰ φιάλας . . . .

Hippolytus *De Antichristo* XXV–XXVI.

HIPPOLYTUS (c. A. D. 170–236)
78

Isaiah, then, prophesies these things. But let us see if John uttered things similar to " his." For this man, being in the island of Patmos, " saw " a revelation of awe-inspiring mysteries, which he relates unreservedly and teaches [to] others. Tell me, O blessed John, Apostle and pupil of the Lord, what have you seen and what have you heard about Babylon?—awake and speak, for she also banished you. "And there came one of the seven angels, who had the seven vials . . . ."[1]

[1] Rev. 17 : 1 and 21 : 9.

III. CANON

LITERATURE

A. H. Charteris, *Canonicity, A Collection of early Testimonies to the Canonical Books of the New Testament*, Edinburgh and London, 1880.

F. W. Grosheide, *Algemene Canoniek van het Nieuwe Testament*, Amsterdam, 1935.

M. R. James, *The Apocryphal New Testament*, Oxford, 1926.

Le P. M.-J. Lagrange, *Histoire ancienne du canon du Nouveau Testament (Études Bibliques, Introduction a l'étude du Nouveau Testament* 1. partie), Paris, 1933.

Johannes Leipoldt, *Geschichte neutestamentlichen Kanons*, 2 Bände, Leipzig, 1907–1908.

A. Loisy, *Histoire du canon du Nouveau Testament*, Paris, 1891.

Alfred Resch, *Agrapha aussercanonische Schriftfragmente gesammelt und untersucht und in zweiter völlig neu bearbeiteter durch alttestamentliche Agrapha vermehrter Auflage. (Texte und Untersuchungen zur Geschichte der altchristlichen Literatur,* herausgegeben von Oscar von Gebhardt und Adolf von Harnack, Neue Folge, XV. Band, 3/4 Heft), Leipzig, 1906.

Alfred Resch, *Die Logia Jesu, nach dem griechischen und hebräischen Text wiederhergestellt*, Leipzig, 1898.

Brooke Foss Westcott, *A General Survey of the History of the Canon of the New Testament*, 7th edition, London, 1896.

Theodor Zahn et al., *Forschungen zur Geschichte des neutestamentlichen Kanons und der altkirchlichen Literatur*, 9 Bände, Erlangen und Leipzig, 1881–1916.

Logion Freerianum

79

Κἀκεῖνοι ἀπελογοῦντο λέγοντες ὅτι ὁ αἰὼν οὗτος τῆς ἀνομίας καὶ τῆς ἀπιστίας ὑπὸ τὸν σατανᾶν ἐστιν, ὁ μὴ ἐῶν τὰ ὑπὸ τῶν πνευμάτων ἀκάθαρτα τὴν ἀλήθειαν τοῦ θεοῦ καταλαβέσθαι δύναμιν· διὰ τοῦτο ἀποκάλυψόν σου τὴν δικαιοσύνην ἤδη ἐκεῖνοι ἔλεγον τῷ χριστῷ· καὶ ὁ χριστὸς ἐκείνοις προσέλεγεν ὅτι πεπλήρωται ὁ ὅρος τῶν ἐτῶν τῆς ἐξουσίας τοῦ σατανᾶ, ἀλλὰ ἐγγίζει ἄλλα δεινά· καὶ ὑπὲρ ὧν ἐγὼ ἁμαρτησάντων παρεδόθην εἰς θάνατον, ἵνα ὑποστρέψωσιν εἰς τὴν ἀλήθειαν καὶ μηκέτι ἁμαρτήσωσιν, ἵνα τὴν ἐν τῷ οὐρανῷ πνευματικὴν καὶ ἄφθαρτον τῆς δικαιοσύνης δόξαν κληρονομήσωσιν. ἀλλὰ πορευθέντες κτλ.

Freer MS. (W.)

Hieronimus

80

In quibusdam exemplaribus et maxime in Graecis codicibus juxta Marcum in fine eius euangelii scribitur Postea cum accubuissent undecim apparuit eis Jesus et exprobravit incredulitatem et duritiam cordis eorum, quia his qui viderant eum resurgentem non crediderunt. et illi satisfaciebant dicentes Saeculum istud iniquitatis et incredulitatis sub Satana est, qui non sinit per immundos spiritus veram Dei apprehendi virtutem. idcirco iam nunc revela iustitiam tuam.

Hieronymus *Adu. Pelag.* II.15.

1. The Ending of Mark

THE FREER LOGION[1]

79

And they excused themselves saying: "This age of iniquity[2] and unbelief is under Satan who does not permit the unclean things that [are] under the spirits to comprehend the truth and power of God.[3] On this account," they said to Christ, "Reveal now thy righteousness." And Christ said to them: "The limit of the years of the authority of Satan has been fulfilled; but other terrible things are drawing near. And on behalf of those who have sinned, I was delivered to death, in order that they might turn to the truth and sin no more, in order that they might inherit the spiritual and incorruptible glory of righteousness which is in heaven. But go...."

[1]Addition to Mk. 16 between verses 14 and 15 in the Codex W, a fifth century MS.
[2]Literally "lawlessness."
[3]Or "who does not permit the things made unclean by the spirits to comprehend the true power of God."

C. R. Gregory, *Das Freerlogion*, Leipzig, 1908.

JEROME

80

In certain exemplars, and especially in the Greek manuscripts [of the Gospel] according to Mark, at the end of his Gospel, there is written: "Afterward, when the Eleven sat at meat, Jesus appeared to them and upbraided [them with] their unbelief and hardness of heart because they had not believed them that had seen Him after His "resurrection." And they made excuse saying: 'This age of iniquity and unbelief is under Satan who does not permit, through unclean spirits, that the true power of God be apprehended. Therefore, reveal even now thy righteousness.'"

81

Πάντα δὲ τὰ παρηγγελμένα τοῖς περὶ τὸν Πέτρον συντόμως ἐξήγγειλαν. μετὰ δὲ ταῦτα καὶ αὐτὸς ὁ Ἰησοῦς ἀπὸ ἀνατολῆς καὶ ἄχρι δύσεως ἐξαπέστειλεν δι' αὐτῶν τὸ ἱερὸν καὶ ἄφθαρτον κήρυγμα τῆς αἰωνίου σωτηρίας.

MSS. L et al.

Agrapha
82

Πάντα ὑπέδειξα ὑμῖν, ὅτι οὕτως κοπιῶντας δεῖ ἀντιλαμβάνεσθαι τῶν ἀσθενούντων, μνημονεύειν τε τῶν λόγων τοῦ κυρίου Ἰησοῦ, ὅτι αὐτὸς εἶπεν Μακάριόν ἐστιν μᾶλλον διδόναι ἢ λαμβάνειν.

Acta Ap. 20.35.

83

Λέγει Ἰ[ησοῦς .... Τίνες] οἱ ἕλκοντες ἡμᾶς [εἰς τὴν βασιλείαν εἰ] ἡ βασιλεία ἐν οὐρα[νῷ ἐστιν; ....]τὰ πετεινὰ τοῦ οὐρ[ανοῦ καὶ τῶν θηρίων ὅ]τι ὑπὸ τὴν γῆν ἐστ[ιν ἢ ἐπὶ τῆς γῆς καὶ] οἱ ἰχθύες τῆς θαλά[σσης οὗτοι οἱ ἕλκον]τες ὑμᾶς, καὶ ἡ βασ[ιλεία τῶν οὐρανῶν] ἐντὸς ὑμῶν [ἐ]στι [καὶ ὅστις ἂν ἑαυτὸν] γνῷ ταύτην εὑρή[σει ....] ἑαυτοὺς γνώσεσθε [καὶ εἰδήσετε ὅτι υἱοί]ἐστε ὑμεῖς τοῦ πατρὸς τοῦ τ[....]γνώσ⟨εσ⟩θε ἑαυτοὺς ἐν[....]καὶ ὑμεῖς ἐστὲ ηπτο[....]

B. P. Grenfell and A. S. Hunt, "Theological Fragments," *The Oxyrhynchus Papyri*, Vol. IV (Oxford, 1904), p. 5f. (Second Saying).

84

Λέγει Ἰη(σοῦ)ς [Πᾶν τὸ μὴ ἔμπροσ]θεν τῆς ὄψεως σου καὶ [τὸ κεκρυμμένον] ἀπὸ σοῦ ἀποκαλυφ⟨θ⟩ήσετ[αί σοι. οὐ γάρ ἐσ]τιν κρυπτὸν ὃ οὐ φανε[ρὸν γενήσεται] καὶ τεθαμμένον ὃ ο[ὐκ ἐγερθήσεται].

Ibid., Fourth Saying, p. 8.

THE SHORT ENDING OF MARK[1]

81

["And they went out and fled from the sepulchre, for fear and astonishment had come upon them; and they said nothing to anyone, for they were afraid."][2]

But all the things that had been commanded they announced briefly to those with Peter. But after these things, Jesus himself also sent forth through them from the East " as far as " to the West the sacred and incorruptible preaching of eternal salvation.

[1] In certain MSS after Mk. 16 : 8, instead of or together with the Lond Ending (Mk. 16 : 9–20). Found in some MSS of the Gospel, cf. Nestle, *Novum Testamentum Graece, ad loc.*   [2] Mk. 16 : 8.

2. Agrapha

82

In all things I have given you an example that so laboring you ought to help the weak, and remember the words of the Lord Jesus, how He himself said: " It is more blessed to give than to receive."

83

Jesus says: ". . . who are *the ones who draw us* to the Kingdom, if *the Kingdom* is *in heaven*? . . . *the winged ones of he*aven, and [×of×] the creatures th*at are under the earth*, or upon the earth, and *the fishes of the sea*, these are drawi*ng you, and the K*ingdom of Heaven *is within you*, and whosoever would *know* himself shall *find it . . . . Know yourselves* and you shall experience that *you are* sons *of the Father, who . . . . Know yourselves . . . and you are . . . .*"

84

Jesus says: " Everything that is not befor*e your face and* that which is hidden *from you, shall be revealed* to you. For there *is* nothing *hidden that* shall not become *manifest and buried that* shall *n*ot be raised up."

85

Πάντα δὲ ὅσα ἐὰν θελήσῃς μὴ γίνεσθαί σοι, καὶ σὺ ἄλλῳ μὴ ποίει.

Didache I.2, cf. Lk. 6:31.

86

Μεμνήμεθα τοῦ κυρίου ἡμῶν καὶ διδασκάλου, ὡς ἐντελλόμενος εἶπεν ἡμῖν· τὰ μυστήρια ἐμοὶ καὶ τοῖς υἱοῖς τοῦ οἴκου μου φυλάξατε.

Clementina XIX.20, cf. I Cor. 4:1 sq.

87

Ὅτι λέγει κύριος Ἀγάπη καλύπτει πλῆθος ἁμαρτιῶν.

Didascalia II.3, cf. I Pt. 4:8; Clemens Alexandrinus Paedagogus III.12.91.

88

Λέγει δὲ κύριος. Ἰδοὺ, ποιῶ τὰ ἔσχατα ὡς τὰ πρῶτα.

Barnabas VI.13, cf. Apoc 21:4 sq.

Euangelion Petri

89

V. Ἦν δὲ μεσημβρία, καὶ σκότος κατέσχε πᾶσαν τὴν Ἰουδαίαν· καὶ ἐθορυβοῦντο καὶ ἠγωνίων μήποτε ὁ ἥλιος ἔδυ ἐπειδὴ ἔτι ἔζη· γέγραπται [γὰρ] αὐτοῖς ἥλιον μὴ δῦναι ἐπὶ πεφονευμένῳ. καί τις αὐτῶν εἶπεν Ποτίσατε αὐτὸν χολὴν μετὰ ὄξους· καὶ κεράσαντες ἐπότισαν. καὶ ἐπλήρωσαν πάντα, καὶ ἐτελείωσαν κατὰ τῆς κεφαλῆς αὐτῶν τὰ ἁμαρτήματα. περιήρχοντο δὲ πολλοὶ μετὰ λύχνων, νομίζοντες ὅτι νύξ ἐστιν· [τινὲς δὲ] ἐπέσαντο. Καὶ ὁ κύριος ἀνεβόησε λέγων Ἡ δύναμίς μου, ἡ δύναμις, κατέλειψάς με· καὶ εἰπὼν ἀνελήφθη καὶ αὐτῆς [καὶ ἐνάτης] ὥρας διεράγη τὸ καταπέτασμα τοῦ ναοῦ τῆς Ἰερουσαλὴμ εἰς δύο.

VI. καὶ τότε ἀπέσπασαν τοὺς ἥλους ἀπὸ τῶν χειρῶν τοῦ κυρίου,

85

"But all whatsoever you would not wish to happen to you, do not you do it to another."

86

We have remembered our Lord and Master how He, commanding us, said: "Keep the mysteries for me and for the sons of my house."

87

That the Lord says: "Love covers a multitude of sins."

88

But the Lord says: "Behold, I make the last things [to be] as the first."

Charles Taylor, *The Oxyrhynchus Logia and the Apocryphal Gospels*, Oxford, 1899; B. P. Grenfell and A. S. Hunt, *The Oxyrynchus Papryi*, Part IV (Oxford, 1904), pp. 1–22.

3. Apocryphal and Canonical Gospels

THE GOSPEL OF PETER (c. A.D. 120–140)

89

a   V. And it was midday and darkness covered all Judea; and they were disturbed and filled with anguish lest the sun had set, since He was still alive; [for] it is written to them that the sun should not go down upon one who had been put to death. And a certain one of them said: "Give Him to drink gall with vinegar." And having mixed it, they gave [Him] to drink. And they fulfilled all things and completed their sins upon their head. But many went about with lamps, thinking that it was night. [And some] fell. And the Lord cried, saying: "My power, [my] power, thou hast left me." And having said [this], He was taken up. And at that very hour, [the ninth], the curtain of the temple in Jerusalem was rent in twain.

VI. And then they drew out the nails from the hands of the

καὶ ἔθηκαν αὐτὸν ἐπὶ τῆς γῆς· καὶ ἡ γῆ πᾶσα ἐσείσθη καὶ φόβος μέγας ἐγένετο. τότε ἥλιος ἔλαμψε καὶ εὑρέθη ὥρα ἐνάτη. ἐχάρησαν δὲ οἱ Ἰουδαῖοι καὶ δεδώκασι τῷ Ἰωσὴφ τὸ σῶμα αὐτοῦ ἵνα αὐτὸ θάψῃ, ἐπειδὴ θεασάμενος ἦν ὅσα ἀγαθὰ ἐποίησεν. λαβὼν δὲ τὸν κύριον ἔλουσε καὶ ⟨ἐν⟩είλησε σινδόνι καὶ εἰσήγαγεν εἰς ἴδιον τάφον καλούμενον Κῆπον Ἰωσήφ . . . .

IX. Τῇ δὲ νυκτὶ ᾗ ἐπέφωσκεν ἡ κυριακή, φυλασσόντων τῶν στρατιωτῶν ἀνὰ δύο δύο κατὰ φρουράν, μεγάλη φωνὴ ἐγένετο ἐν τῷ οὐρανῷ καὶ εἶδον ἀνοιχθέντας τοὺς οὐρανοὺς καὶ δύο ἄνδρας κατελθόντας ἐκεῖθεν, πολὺ φέγγος ἔχοντας καὶ ἐγγίσαντας τῷ τάφῳ. ὁ δὲ λίθος ἐκεῖνος ὁ βεβλημένος ἐπὶ τῇ θύρᾳ ἀφ' ἑαυτοῦ κυλισθεὶς ἐπεχώρησε παρὰ μέρος, καὶ ὁ τάφος ἠνοίγη καὶ ἀμφότεροι οἱ νεανίσκοι εἰσῆλθον. ἰδόντες οὖν οἱ στρατιῶται ἐκεῖνοι ἐξύπνισαν τὸν κεντυρίωνα καὶ τοὺς πρεσβυτέρους, παρῆσαν γὰρ καὶ αὐτοὶ φυλάσσοντες· καὶ ἐξηγουμένων αὐτῶν ἃ εἶδον, πάλιν ὁρῶσιν ἐξελθόντας ἀπὸ τοῦ τάφου τρεῖς ἄνδρας, καὶ τοὺς δύο τὸν ἕνα ὑπορθοῦντας, καὶ σταυρὸν ἀκολουθοῦντα αὐτοῖς· καὶ τῶν μὲν δύο τὴν κεφαλὴν χωροῦσαν μέχρι τοῦ οὐρανοῦ, τοῦ δὲ χειραγωγουμένου ὑπ' αὐτῶν ὑπερβαίνουσαν τοὺς οὐρανούς. καὶ φωνῆς ἤκουον ἐκ τῶν οὐρανῶν λεγούσης Ἐκήρυξας τοῖς κοιμωμένοις; καὶ ὑπακοὴ ἠκούετο ἀπὸ τοῦ σταυροῦ τὸ Ναι. Συνεσκέπτοντο οὖν ἀλλήλοις ἐκεῖνοι ἀπελθεῖν καὶ ἐνφανίσαι ταῦτα τῷ Πειλάτῳ . . .

XII. Ὄρθρου δὲ τῆς κυριακῆς Μαριὰμ ἡ Μαγδαληνή, μαθήτρια τοῦ κυρίου, φοβουμένη διὰ τοὺς Ἰουδαίους, ἐπειδὴ ἐφλέγοντο ὑπὸ τῆς ὀργῆς, οὐκ ἐποίησεν ἐπὶ τῷ μνήματι τοῦ κυρίου ἃ εἰώθεσαν ποιεῖν αἱ γυναῖκες ἐπὶ τοῖς ἀποθνήσκουσι καὶ τοῖς ἀγαπωμένοις αὐταῖς, λαβοῦσα μεθ' ἑαυτῆς τὰς φίλας ἦλθε ἐπὶ τὸ μνημεῖον ὅπου ἦν τιθείς. καὶ ἐφοβοῦντο μὴ ἴδωσιν αὐτὰς οἱ Ἰουδαῖοι, καὶ ἔλεγον Εἰ καὶ μὴ ἐν ἐκείνῃ τῇ ἡμέρᾳ ᾗ ἐσταυρώθη ἐδυνήθημεν κλαῦσαι καὶ κόψασθαι, καὶ νῦν ἐπὶ τοῦ μνήματος αὐτοῦ ποιήσωμεν ταῦτα. τίς δὲ ἀποκυλίσει ἡμῖν καὶ τὸν λίθον τὸν τεθέντα ἐπὶ τῆς θύρας τοῦ μνημείου, ἵνα εἰσελθοῦσαι παρακαθεσθῶμεν αὐτῷ καὶ ποιήσωμεν τὰ ὀφειλόμενα; μέγας γὰρ ἦν ὁ λίθος, καὶ φοβούμεθα μή τις ἡμᾶς ἴδῃ. καὶ εἰ μὴ δυνάμεθα, κἂν ἐπὶ τῆς θύρας βάλωμεν ἃ φέρομεν εἰς μνημοσύνην αὐτοῦ, κλαύσομεν καὶ κοψόμεθα ἕως ἔλθωμεν εἰς τὸν οἶκον ἡμῶν. Καὶ ἀπελθοῦσαι εὗρον τὸν τάφον ἠνεῳγμένον· καὶ προσελθοῦσαι παρέκυψαν ἐκεῖ, καὶ ὁρῶσιν ἐκεῖ τινα νεανίσκον

Lord and placed Him upon the earth. And the whole earth was
b shaken and there was great fear. Then the sun shone forth and it was found to be the ninth hour. And the Jews rejoiced; and they gave to Joseph His body to bury, since he had seen what good things He had done. And taking the Lord, he washed [His body] and wrapped it in a linen cloth and brought it to his own tomb called the Garden of Joseph . . . .

IX. But in the night in which the Lord's [Day] dawned, when the soldiers were keeping guard two by two on the watch, there was a tremendous sound in the sky and they saw the heavens opened and two men coming down from thence "radiating" much light and drawing near to the tomb. But that stone which had been placed at the door, rolling by itself, partially moved aside and the tomb was opened and both the young men went in. The[1] soldiers, therefore, seeing [this] woke the centurion and the elders—for they too were present, keeping guard. And while they were telling [them] what they had seen, they "saw" again three men, coming forth from the tomb, and two of them supporting the one and a cross following them, and the head[s] of
c the two reaching unto heaven, but [the head] of Him who was led of them by the hand reaching beyond the heavens. And they heard a voice from the heavens saying: "Didst thou preach to them that sleep?" And a response was heard from the cross: "Yes."

Therefore, they took counsel with one another to go and reveal these things to Pilate . . . .

XII. But early on the Lord's Day Mary Magdalene, a disciple of the Lord—afraid because of the Jews, since they were incensed with anger—did not do at the sepulchre of the Lord the things which women "are" accustomed to do for those who die and are dear to them, [but] taking her friends with her, she came to the sepulchre where He was laid. And they were afraid lest the Jews should see them and kept on saying: "Since we were not even able to weep and lament on that day on which He was crucified, let us now at least do these things at his sepulchre. But who will roll away for us the stone which was placed at the door of the sepulchre, that entering we may sit beside Him and do the things that are required?"—for the stone was very great—" and
d we are afraid lest anyone see us. And if we are not able, even though we cast at the door what we bear in memory of Him, we will weep and lament until we come to our house." And proceeding they found the tomb opened; and coming up they looked in there; and they see there a certain young man sitting

[1] Literally "These."

καθεζόμενον μέσῳ τοῦ τάφου, ὡραῖον καὶ περιβεβλημένον στολὴν λαμπροτάτην, ὅστις ἔφη αὐταῖς Τί ἤλθατε; τίνα ζητεῖτε; μὴ τὸν σταυρωθέντα ἐκεῖνον; ἀνέστη καὶ ἀπῆλθεν· εἰ δὲ μὴ πιστεύετε, παρακύψατε καὶ ἴδατε τὸν τόπον ἔνθα ἔκειτο, ὅτι οὐκ ἔστιν· ἀνέστη γὰρ καὶ ἀπῆλθεν ἐκεῖ ὅθεν ἀπεστάλη. τότε αἱ γυναῖκες φοβηθεῖσαι ἔφυγον· ἦν δὲ τελευταία ἡμέρα τῶν ἀζύμων, καὶ πολλοί τινες ἐξήρχοντο, ὑποστρέφοντες εἰς τοὺς οἴκους αὐτῶν τῆς ἑορτῆς παυσαμένης.

XIV. Ἡμεῖς δὲ οἱ δώδεκα μαθηταὶ τοῦ κυρίου ἐκλαίομεν καὶ ἐλυπούμεθα, καὶ ἕκαστος λυπούμενος διὰ τὸ συμβὰν ἀπηλλάγη εἰς τὸν οἶκον αὐτοῦ. ἐγὼ δὲ Σίμων Πέτρος καὶ Ἀνδρέας ὁ ἀδελφός μου λαβόντες ἡμῶν τὰ λίνα ἀπήλθαμεν εἰς τὴν θάλασσαν· καὶ ἦν σὺν ἡμῖν Λευεὶς ὁ τοῦ Ἁλφαίου, ὃν Κύριος * * * *

Euangelion Petri V–VI, IX–X, XII–XIV, cf. Eusebius H.E. III.3 et 25; Hieronymus De uir. inl. I.

Origen

90

Ἐὰν δὲ προσιῆταί τις τὸ καθ᾽ Ἑβραίους εὐαγγέλιον, ἔνθα αὐτὸς ὁ σωτήρ φησιν Ἄρτι ἔλαβέ με ἡ μήτηρ μου κτλ. ἐπαπορήσει πῶς μήτηρ Χριστοῦ τὸ διὰ τοῦ λόγου γεγενημένον πνεῦμα ἅγιον εἶναι δύναται.

Origen In Iohan. II.87.

Hieronymus

91

In euangelio juxta Hebraeos, quod Chaldaico quidem Syroque sermone, sed Hebraicis litteris scriptum est, quo utuntur usque hodie Nazareni, secundum Apostolos, siue ut plerique autumant, juxta Matthaeum, quod et in Caesariensi habetur bibliotheca, narrat historia Ecce mater Domini et fratres eius dicebant ei Iohannes Baptista baptizat in remissionem peccatorum: eamus et baptizemur ab eo. dixit autem eis Quid peccaui, ut uadam et baptizer ab eo? nisi forte hoc ipsum quod dixi, ignorantia est.

Hieronymus Adu. Pelag. III.2.

in the midst of the tomb, beautiful and clothed with a very bright garment, who said to them: " Why did you come: Whom do you seek? Not that one who was crucified? He is risen and is gone away. But if you do not believe, "look" and see the place where he was laid, that he is not [here]. For he is risen and is gone there whence he was sent." Then the women, being afraid, fled. And it was the last day of Unleavened Bread and many were departing, returning to their houses, the feast being over.

XII. But we, the twelve disciples of the Lord, wept and were grieved, and each being grieved because of what had come to pass departed to his house. But I, Simon Peter, and Andrew, my brother, taking our lines[1] went away to the sea; and there was with us Levi, the son of Alphaeus, whom the Lord . . . .

[1] I.e. nets.

A. Harnack, *Bruckstücke des Evangeliums und der Apokalypse des Petrus*, 2. verbesserte und erweiterte Auflage, Leipzig, 1893; H. v. Schubert, *The Gospel of St. Peter. Synoptical Tables, with Translation and Critical Apparatus*, Edinburgh, 1893; J. R. Harris, *The Newly-Recovered Gospel of St. Peter, with a Full Account of the Same*, New York, 1893; C. H. Turner, " The Gospel of Peter," *The Journal of Theol. Stud.*, 14 (1913), pp. 161-195; H. Stocks, " Quellen zur Rekonstruktion des Petrusevangeliums," *Zeitschr. f. Kirchengesch.*, 34 (1913), pp. 1-57; L. Vaganay, *L'Évangile de Pierre*. Paris, 1930.

ORIGEN

90

But if someone would accept the Gospel according to the Hebrews, where the Saviour himself says: " Recently my mother took me etc.," he will be perplexed as to how the mother of Christ could be the Holy Spirit which came through the Word.

JEROME

91

In the Gospel according to the Hebrews which is written in the Chaldee and Syriac language but in Hebrew letters, which the Nazarenes use even today [as the Gospel] according to the Apostles or, as many affirm, [the Gospel] according to Matthew, which is contained in the library at Caesarea, the narrative says: " Behold, the mother of our Lord and His brethren said to Him: ' John the Baptist is baptizing for the remission of sins; let us go and be baptized by him.' But He said to them: ' In what have I sinned, that I should go and be baptized by him, unless this thing that I have said is ignorance?' "

92

Porro in evangelio, cuius supra fecimus mentionem, haec scripta reperimus Factum est autem cum ascendisset Dominus de aqua, descendit fons omnis Spiritus sancti, et requieuit super eum, et dixit illi Fili mi, in omnibus prophetis exspectabam te, ut uenires, et requiescerem in te. tu es enim requies mea, tu es filius meus primogenitus, qui regnas in sempiternum.

Hieronymus *In Isa.* XI.2.

93

Hic est de quo et apostolus Paulus scribit ad Galatas Alium autem apostolorum uidi neminem nisi Iacobum fratrem Domini; et apostolorum super hoc crebrius Acta testantur, euangelium quoque quod appellatur secundum Hebraeos et a me nuper in Graecum sermonem Latinumque translatum est, quo et Origenes saepe utitur, post resurrectionem Salvatoris refert Dominus autem cum dedisset sindonem seruo sacerdotis, iuit ad Iacobum et apparuit ei—iurauerat enim Iacobus se non comesurum panem ab illa hora qua biberat calicem Domini, donec uideret eum resurgentem a dormientibus—rursusque post paululum, Adferte, ait Dominus, mensam et panem, statimque additur Tulit panem et benedixit et fregit et dedit Iacobo Iusto et dixit ei Frater mi, comede panem tuum, quia resurrexit filius hominis a dormientibus.

Hieronymus *De uir. inl.* II, cf. III; Origen *In Iohan.* II. 87 (no. 90); Irenaeus *Adu. haer.* I.26.2; Clemens Alexandrinus *Stromata* II.9.45.

92

Further in the Gospel of which we have made mention above,[1] we find these things written: "And it came to pass when the Lord had ascended from the water that the whole fount of the Holy Spirit descended and rested upon Him and said to Him: ' My son, in all the prophets I was looking for you to come that I may rest in you. For you are my rest; you are my first born son who reignest forever.' "

[1] I.e. The Gospel according to the Hebrews.

93

This is he concerning whom the Apostle Paul also writes to the Galatians: " But I saw none other of the Apostles except James, the brother of the Lord;" and concerning this one the Acts of the Apostles bears witness rather frequently; also the Gospel, which is called According to the Hebrews—and [which] was recently translated by me into the Greek and Latin language[s], which Origen also frequently uses—reports [as follows] subsequent to the resurrection of the Saviour: " But the Lord, when he had given the linen garment to the servant of the priest, went to James and appeared to him—for James had sworn that he would not eat bread from that hour in which he drank the cup of the Lord, until he should see Him rising from them that sleep." And again, after a little [it continues]: " Bring," says the Lord, " a table and bread;" and immediately there is added: " He took up bread and blessed and broke and gave to James Justus and said to him: ' My brother, eat thy bread, for the Son of Man has risen from them that sleep.' "

E. B. Nicholson, *The Gospel according to the Hebrews*, London, 1879; Rud. Handmann, *Das Hebräer Evangelium* (T. u. U., V. Band, 3. Heft), 1888; Edgar J. Goodspeed, *A History of early Christian Literature*, (Chicago, 1944), pp. 66–73. For summary of views: M. H. Shepherd, " Paul and the Double Resurrection Tradition " (plus appended note), *Journal of Biblical Literature*, 64, 2 (1945), pp. 227–240.

Irenaeus

94

Καὶ οὐ μόνον ἐκ τῶν εὐαγγελικῶν καὶ τῶν ἀποστολικῶν πειρῶνται τὰς ἀποδείξεις ποιεῖσθαι, παρατρέποντες τὰς ἑρμηνείας, καὶ ῥᾳδιουργοῦντες τὰς ἐξηγήσεις· ἀλλὰ καὶ ἐκ νόμου καὶ προφητῶν ....

Irenaeus *Adu. haer.* I.3.6.

95

Neque autem plura numero quam haec sunt neque rursus pauciora capit esse euangelia. ἐπειδὴ [γὰρ] τέσσαρα κλίματα τοῦ κόσμου, ἐν ᾧ ἐσμέν, εἰσιν καὶ τέσσαρα καθολικὰ πνεύματα, κατέσπαρται δὲ ἡ ἐκκλησία ἐπὶ πάσης τῆς γῆς, στῦλος δὲ καὶ στήριγμα ἐκκλησίας τὸ εὐαγγέλιον καὶ πνεῦμα ζωῆς· εἰκότως τέσσαρας ἔχειν αὐτὴν στύλους, πανταχόθεν πνέοντας τὴν ἀφθαρσίαν καὶ ἀναζωπυροῦντας τοὺς ἀνθρώπους.

Irenaeus *Adu. haer.* III.11.8.

Canon Muratorianus

96

(*Original*)

quibus tamen interfuit et ita posuit· tertio euangelii librum secundo lucan lucas iste medicus post ascensum x̄p̄i. cum eo paulus quasi ut iuris studiosum secundum adsumsisset numeni suo ex opinione concripset d̄n̄m̄ tamen nec ipse ḍ uidit in carne et idē prout asequi potuit· ita et ad natiuitate iohannis incipet dicere, quarti euangeliorum iohannis ex decipolis cohortantibus condescipulis et ēp̄s̄ suis dixit conieiunate

(*Restored*)

quibus tamen interfuit et ita posuit. tertium euangelii librum secundum Lucam. Lucas iste medicus post ascensum Christi cum eum Paulus quasi itineris sui socium secum adsumsisset nomine suo ex opinione conscripsit—Dominum tamen nec ipse uidit in carne—et idem prout assequi potuit: ita et a natiuitate Iohannis incepit dicere. quarti euangeliorum Iohannis ex discipulis. cohortantibus condiscipulis et episcopis suis

IRENAEUS

94

And they[1] attempt not only to "obtain" proofs from the "Evangelists" and the "Apostles," distorting the versions and making light of the expositions, but they [quote] also from the Law and Prophets . . . .

[1]The gnostics.

95

And it is impossible that the Gospels can be either more in number or, on the other hand, less than they are. For since there are four zones of the world in which we are, and also four principal winds, and [since] the Church is scattered throughout the whole world, and since the pillar and support of the Church is the Gospel and the Spirit of life, it is natural that she should have four pillars breathing out immortality all over and rekindling men.

4. Canonical Lists

THE MURATORIAN CANON (c. A. D. 170-190)[1]

96

a But he was present among them,[2] and so he put [the facts down in his Gospel.] The third book of the Gospel [is that] according to Luke. Luke, "the" physician, after the ascension of Christ, when Paul had taken him with him as a companion of his traveling, [and after he had made] an investigation, wrote in his own name—but neither did he see the Lord in the flesh—and thus, as he was able to investigate, so he also begins to tell the story [starting] from the nativity of John. The fourth [book] of the Gospels is that of John [one] of the disciples. When his fellow-disciples and bishops urged [him], he said: "Fast to-

[1]Published by Muratori in 1740 from an eighth century MS.
[2]Or "And he was present at these deeds," but less likely.

mihi· odie triduo et quid cuique fuerit reuelatum alterutrum nobis ennarremus eadem nocte reuelatum andreae ex apostolis ut recogniscentibus cuntis iohannis suo nomine cuncta discriberet et ideo licit uaria sinculis euangeliorum libris principia doceantur nihil tamen differt credentium fidei cum uno ac principali s̄pū declarate sint in omnibus omnia de natiuitate de passione de resurrectione de conuersatione cum decipulis suis ac de gemino eius aduentu primo in humilitate dispectus quod fφtµ secundum potestate regali preclarum quod foturum est. quid ergo mirum si iohannes tam constanter sincula etīa in epistulis suis proferam dicens in semeipsu quae uidimus oculis nostris et auribus audiuimus et manus nostrae palpauerunt haec scripsimus uobis sic enim non solum uisurem sed & auditorem sed & scriptorē omnium mirabiliū d̄n̄i per ordinem profetetur acta autē omniū apostolorum sub uno libro scribta sunt lucas obtime theofile conprindit quia sub praesentia eius singula gerebantur sicut¢ et semote passionē petri euidenter declarat sed & profectionē pauli ab urbe ad spaniā proficescentis epistulae autem pauli

dixit Conıeıunate mihi hodie triduum, et quid cuique fuerit reuelatum alterutrum nobis enarremus. eadem nocte reuelatum Andreae ex apostolis, ut recognoscentibus cunctis, Iohannes suo nomine cuncta describeret. et ideo licet varia singulis euangeliorum libris principia doceantur nihil tamen differt credentium fidei, cum uno ac principali spiritu declarata sint in omnibus omnia de natiuitate, de passione, de resurrectione de conuersatione cum discipulis suis, et de gemino eius aduentu, primum in humilitate despectus, quod fuit, secundum potestate regali praeclarum, quod futurum est. quid ergo mirum, si Iohannes tam constanter singula etiam in epistolis suis proferat dicens in semetipso[1] Quae uidimus oculis nostris, et auribus audiuimus, et manus nostrae palpauerunt, haec scripsimus uobis? Sic enim non solum uisorem, sed et auditorem, sed et scriptorem omnium mirabilium Domini per ordinem profitetur.

Acta autem omnium apostolorum sub uno libro scripta sunt. Lucas "optimo Theophilo" comprehendit, quae sub praesentia eius singula gerebantur, sicut et remote[2] passionem Petri evidenter declarat, sed et profectionem Pauli ab urbe ad Spaniam proficiscentis.

---

[1] *Semetipsum* suggested by Westcott.
[2] Westcott: *semota...declarant.* Hilgenfeld: *semota passione Petri declarat sed et profectione Pauli.* Routh: *remota... declarant.* Charteris: *semote.*

gether with me today for three days and, what shall be revealed to each, let us tell [it] to each other." On the same night it was revealed to Andrew, [one] of the Apostles, that, with all of them reviewing [it], John should describe all things in his own name.

b And so, although different beginnings might be taught in the separate books of the Gospels, nevertheless it makes no difference to the faith of believers, since all things in all [of them] are declared by the one sovereign Spirit—concerning [His] nativity, concerning [His] passion, concerning [His] resurrection, concerning [His] walk with His disciples, and concerning His double advent: the first in humility when He was despised, which has been; the second in royal power, glorious, which is to be. What marvel, therefore, if John so constantly brings forward particular [matters] also in his Epistles, saying of himself: " What we have seen with our eyes and have heard with [our] ears and our hands have handled, these things we have written to you."[1] For thus he declares that he was not only an eyewitness and hearer, but also a writer of all the wonderful things of the Lord in order.

c The Acts of all the Apostles, however, were written in one volume. Luke described briefly " for " most excellent Theophilus particular [things], which happened in his presence, as he also evidently relates indirectly the death of Peter (?) and also Paul's departure from the city as he was proceeding to Spain.

[1] Jn. 1 : 1.

quae a quo loco uel qua ex causa directe sint uolentatibus intellegere ipse declarant primū omnium corintheis scysmae heresis interdicens deinceps ℏ callatis circumcisione romanis autē orp̄dine scripturarum sed et principium earum φtd esse x̄p̄m̄ intimans prolexius scripsit de quibus sincolis necesse est ad nobis desputari cum ipse beatus apostolus paulus sequens prodecessuris sui iohannis ordinē non nisi nomenati semptaē ecclesiis scribat ordine tali a corenthios prima. ad efesius seconda ad philippinses tertia ad colosensis quarta ad calatas quinta ad tensaolenecinsis sexta· ad romanos septima uerum corentheis et thesaolecensibus licet pro correbtione iteretur una tamen per omnem orbem terrae ecclesia deffusa esse denoscitur et iohannis enì in apocalebsy licet septē eccleseis scribat tamen omnibus dicit uerū ad filemonem una' et at titū una et ad tymotheū duas pro affecto et dilectione in honore tamen eclesiae catholice in ordinatione eclesiastice descepline s̄c̄ificate sunt. Fertur etiam ad laudecenses alia ad alexandrinos pauli nomine fincte ad heresem marcionis et alia plura quae in chatholicam eclesiam recepi non potest fel enim cum melle misceri non concruit epistola sane iude et superscrictio iohannis duas in catholica habentur et sapientia ab amicis salomonis in honorē ipsius scripta apocalapse

Epistolae autem Pauli, quae, a quo loco, uel qua ex causa directae sint, uolentibus intellegere ipsae declarant. primum omnium Corinthiis schisma haeresis interdicens, deinceps Galatis circumcisionem, Romanis autem ordine scripturarum, sed et principium earum esse Christum intimans, prolixius scripsit; de quibus singulis necesse est a nobis disputari; cum ipse beatus Apostolus Paulus sequens prodecessoris sui Iohannis ordinem, nonnisi nominatim septem ecclesiis scribat ordine tali: ad Corinthios prima, ad Ephesios secunda, ad Philippenses tertia, ad Colossenses quarta, ad Galatas quinta, ad Thessalonicensibus sexta, ad Romanos septima. uerum Corinthiis, et Thessalonicensibus licet pro correptione iteretur, una tamen per omnem orbem terrae ecclesia diffusa esse denoscitur. et Iohannes enim in Apocalypsi licet septem ecclesiis scribat, tamen omnibus dicit. uerum ad Philemonem unam, et ad Titum unam, et ad Timotheum duas pro affectu et dilectione; in honore tamen ecclesiae catholicae, in ordinatione ecclesiasticae disciplinae sanctificatae sunt. fertur etiam ad Laodicenses, alia ad Alexandrinos, Pauli nomine fictae ad haeresem Marcionis, et alia plura, quae in catholicam ecclesiam recipi non potest; fel enim cum melle misceri non congruit.

Epistola sane Iudae, et superscriptio Iohannis duas in catholica habentur; et Sapientia ab amicis Salomonis in honorem ipsius

The Epistles of Paul themselves, however, show to those, who wish to know, which [they are], from what place, and for what cause they were sent. First of all he wrote to the Corinthians, admonishing against schism of heresy; thereupon to the Galatians [admonishing against] circumcision; to the Romans, however, [he wrote] rather lengthily pointing out with a series of Scripture quotations that Christ is their main theme also (?) [But] it is necessary that we have a discussion singly concerning these, since the blessed Apostle Paul himself, imitating the example of his predecessor, John, wrote to seven churches only by name *d* [and] in this order: The first [Epistle] to the Corinthians, the second to the Ephesians, the third to the Philippians, the fourth to the Colossians, the fifth to the Galatians, the sixth to the Thessalonians, and the seventh to the Romans. But, although he wrote twice to the Corinthians and to the Thessalonians, for reproof (?), nevertheless [it is evident that] one Church is made known to be diffused throughout the whole globe of the earth. For John also, though he wrote in the Apocalypse to seven churches, nevertheless he speaks to them all. But he [wrote] one [letter] to Philemon and one to Titus, but two to Timothy for the sake of affection and love. In honor[1] of the General Church, however, they have been sanctified by an ordination of the ecclesiastical discipline. There is extant also [an epistle] to the Laodiceans, and another to the Alexandrians, forged in the name of Paul according to the heresy of Marcion. There are also many others which cannot be received in the General Church, for gall cannot be mixed with honey.

[1] Or "by acknowledgment."

etiam iohanis et petri tantum recipimus quam quidam ex nostris legi in eclesia nolunt pastorem uero nuperrim e⸱temporibus nostris in urbe roma herma conscripsit sedente cathetra urbis romae aeclesiae pio ēps fratreṭ eius et ideo legi eum quidē oportet se puplicare uero in eclesia populo neque inter profetas conpletum numero neque inter apostolos in finē temporum potest. arsinoi autem seu ualentini· uel mitiadis nihil in totum recipemus. qui etiam nouū psalmorum librum marcioni conscripserunt una cum basilide assianom catafry cum constitutorem . . . .

scripta. apocalypses etiam Iohannis, et Petri, tantum recipimus, quam quidam ex nostris legi in ecclesia nolunt. Pastorem uero nuperrime temporibus nostris in Urbe Roma Hermas conscripsit, sedente cathedra Urbis Romae ecclesiae Pio Episcopo fratre eius; et ideo legi eum quidem oportet, se publicare uero in ecclesia populo, neque inter Prophetas, completum numero, neque inter apostolos, in finem temporum potest.

Arsinoi autem, seu Ualentini, uel Mitiadis nihil in totum recipimus. qui etiam nouum Psalmorum librum Marcioni concripserunt una cum Basilide Assianum Catafrygum constitutorem . . . .

Cf. A. H. Charteris, *Canonicity*, pp. 5–8.

Origen

97

Ἐν δὲ τῷ πρώτῳ τῶν εἰς τὸ κατὰ Ματθαῖον, τὸν ἐκκλησιαστικὸν φυλάττων κανόνα, μόνα τέσσαρα εἰδέναι εὐαγγέλια μαρτύρεται, ὧδέ πως γράφων Ὡς ἐν παραδόσει μαθὼν περὶ τῶν τεσσάρων εὐαγγελίων, ἃ καὶ μόνα ἀναντίρρητά ἐστιν ἐν τῇ ὑπὸ τὸν οὐρανὸν ἐκκλησίᾳ τοῦ θεοῦ, ὅτι πρῶτον μὲν γέγραπται τὸ κατὰ τόν ποτε τελώνην, ὕστερον δὲ ἀπόστολον Ἰησοῦ Χριστοῦ Ματθαῖον, ἐκδεδωκότα αὐτὸ τοῖς ἀπὸ Ἰουδαϊσμοῦ πιστεύσασιν, γράμμασιν Ἑβραϊκοῖς συντεταγμένον· δεύτερον δὲ τὸ κατὰ Μάρκον, ὡς Πέτρος ὑφηγήσατο αὐτῷ, ποιήσαντα, ὃν καὶ υἱὸν ἐν τῇ καθολικῇ ἐπιστολῇ διὰ τούτων ὡμολόγησεν φάσκων Ἀσπάζεται ὑμᾶς ἡ ἐν βαβυλῶνι συνεκλεκτὴ καὶ Μάρκος ὁ υἱός μου· καὶ τρίτον τὸ κατὰ Λουκᾶν, τὸ ὑπὸ Παύλου ἐπαινούμενον εὐαγγέλιον τοῖς ἀπὸ τῶν ἐθνῶν πεποιηκότα· ἐπὶ πᾶσιν τὸ κατὰ Ἰωάννην.

e   The Epistle of Jude indeed and the two with the superscription, "Of John," are accepted in the General [Church]—so also the Wisdom of Solomon written by friends in his honor. We accept only the Apocalypses of John and of Peter, although some of us do not want it[1] to be read in the Church. But Hermas composed The Shepherd quite recently in our times in the city of Rome, while his brother, Pius, the bishop, occupied the [episcopal] seat of the city of Rome. And therefore, it should indeed be read, but it cannot be published for the people in the Church, neither among the Prophets, since their number is complete, nor among the Apostles for it is after their time (?).

But we accept nothing at all of Arsinoes, or Valentinus, or Metiades (?). Those also [are rejected] who composed a new book of Psalms for Marcion together with Basilides and the Cataphrygians of Asia (?)....

ORIGEN

97

a   In the first of the [books] on the [Gospel] according to Matthew, observing the ecclesiastical canon, he testifies that he knows only four Gospels, writing somewhat as follows, " as he has learned by tradition concerning the four Gospels, which alone are undisputed in the Church of God under heaven, that first there was written the [Gospel] according to Matthew, the one-time publican but afterwards an Apostle of Jesus Christ, who published it in the Hebrew language for those from Judaism who believed; and that secondly, there [was written] the [Gospel] according to Mark, who made it as Peter instructed him, whom also he acknowledges as son in the Catholic Epistle in these [words] saying: ' The [Church] in Babylon, elect together [with you] and Mark, my son, salute you ';[2] and thirdly, that according to Luke—the Gospel praised by Paul—who made [it] for those from the Gentiles [who believed]; last of all, the [Gospel] according to John [was written]."

[1] The Apocalypse of Peter (?), or the second Epistle of Peter.
  S. P. Tregelles, *Canon Muratorianus*, Oxford, 1867; George Milligan, *The New Testament Documents, Their Origin and Early History* (London, 1913), Note K, pp. 287-291; Theodor Zahn, " Hippolytus der Verfasser des Muratorischen Kanons," *Neue Kirchliche Zeitschrift*, XXIII (1922), pp. 417-436; Fr. M.-J. Lagrange, " Le canon d'Hippolyte et le fragment de Muratori," *Revue Biblique*, XLII (1933), pp. 161-186.
[2] I Pet. 5 : 13.

Καὶ ἐν τῷ πέμπτῳ δὲ τῶν εἰς τὸ κατὰ Ἰωάννην Ἐξηγητικῶν ὁ αὐτὸς ταῦτα περὶ τῶν ἐπιστολῶν τῶν ἀποστόλων φησίν· Ὁ δὲ ἱκανωθεὶς διάκονος γενέσθαι τῆς καινῆς διαθήκης, οὐ γράμματος, ἀλλὰ πνεύματος, Παῦλος, ὁ πεπληρωκὼς τὸ εὐαγγέλιον ἀπὸ Ἱερουσαλὴμ καὶ κύκλῳ μέχρι τοῦ Ἰλλυρικοῦ, οὐδὲ πάσαις ἔγραψεν αἷς ἐδίδαξεν ἐκκλησίαις, ἀλλὰ καὶ αἷς ἔγραψεν, ὀλίγους στίχους ἐπέστειλεν. Πέτρος δέ, ἐφ' ᾧ οἰκοδομεῖται ἡ Χριστοῦ ἐκκλησία, ἧς πύλαι Ἅιδου οὐ κατισχύσουσιν, μίαν ἐπιστολὴν ὁμολογουμένην καταλέλοιπεν, ἔστω δὲ καὶ δευτέραν· ἀμφιβάλλεται γάρ. τί δεῖ περὶ τοῦ ἀναπεσόντος ἐπὶ τὸ στῆθος λέγειν τοῦ Ἰησοῦ, Ἰωάννου, ὃς εὐαγγέλιον ἓν καταλέλοιπεν, ὁμολογῶν δύνασθαι τοσαῦτα ποιήσειν ἃ οὐδ' ὁ κόσμος χωρῆσαι ἐδύνατο; ἔγραφεν δὲ καὶ τὴν Ἀποκάλυψιν, κελευσθεὶς σιωπῆσαι καὶ μὴ γράψαι τὰς τῶν ἑπτὰ βροντῶν φωνάς· καταλέλοιπεν καὶ ἐπιστολὴν πάνυ ὀλίγων στίχων, ἔστω δὲ καὶ δευτέραν καὶ τρίτην· ἐπεὶ οὐ πάντες φασὶν γνησίους εἶναι ταύτας· πλὴν οὔκ εἰσιν στίχων ἀμφότεραι ἑκατόν.

Ἔτι πρὸς τούτοις περὶ τῆς Πρὸς Ἑβραίους ἐπιστολῆς ἐν ταῖς εἰς αὐτὴν Ὁμιλίαις ταῦτα διαλαμβάνει . . . .

Origen, cf. Eusebius H.E. VI.25.3–10.

Eusebius

98

Εὔλογον δ' ἐνταῦθα γενομένους ἀνακεφαλαιώσασθαι τὰς δηλωθείσας τῆς καινῆς διαθήκης γραφάς. καὶ δὲ τακτέον ἐν πρώτοις τὴν ἁγίαν τῶν εὐαγγελίων τετρακτύν, οἷς ἕπεται ἡ τῶν Πράξεων τῶν ἀποστόλων γραφή· μετὰ δὲ ταύτην τὰς Παύλου καταλεκτέον ἐπιστολάς, αἷς ἑξῆς τὴν φερομένην Ἰωάννου προτέραν καὶ ὁμοίως τὴν Πέτρου κυρωτέον ἐπιστολήν· ἐπὶ τούτοις τακτέον, εἴ γε φανείη, τὴν Ἀποκάλυψιν Ἰωάννου, περὶ ἧς τὰ δόξαντα κατὰ καιρὸν ἐκθησόμεθα. καὶ ταῦτα μὲν ἐν ὁμολογουμένοις· τῶν δ' ἀντιλεγομένων, γνωρίμων δ' οὖν ὅμως τοῖς πολλοῖς, ἡ λεγομένη Ἰακώβου φέρεται καὶ ἡ Ἰούδα ἥ τε Πέτρου δευτέρα ἐπιστολὴ καὶ ἡ ὀνομαζομένη δευτέρα καὶ τρίτη Ἰωάννου, εἴτε τοῦ εὐαγγελιστοῦ τυγχάνουσαι εἴτε καὶ ἑτέρου ὁμωνύμου ἐκείνῳ. ἐν τοῖς νόθοις κατατετάχθω καὶ τῶν Παύλου Πράξεων ἡ γραφὴ ὅ τε λεγόμενος Ποιμὴν καὶ ἡ

b And in the fifth [book] of the *Expositions on [the Gospel] According to John* the same one expresses these [views] regarding the Epistles of the Apostles: "But he who was made sufficient to become a minister of the new covenant, not of the letter, but of the Spirit,[1] [namely] Paul, who spread the Gospel from Jerusalem and vicinity to Illyricum,[2] did not write to all the churches which he instructed, but to some that he wrote, he sent only a few lines. And Peter on whom the Church of Christ is being built, which the gates of hell shall not overpower,[3] left behind one acknowledged epistle, and, it may be, a second one; for it is doubted. Why should one speak of [him], who reclined on the breast of Jesus, [namely] John, who left behind one Gospel, admitting that he could write so many, as not even the world could contain?[4] He wrote also the Apocalypse, having been ordered to keep silent and not to record the voices of the seven thunders.[5] He left behind an epistle also, of a very few lines; it may be, a second and a third, for not all say that these are genuine. Nevertheless, both together are not a hundred lines."

Further, in addition to these, he separately discusses the following about the Epistle to the Hebrews in his *Homilies* on it . . . .[6]

[1] II Cor. 3 : 6. [2] Rom. 15 : 19. [3] Mt. 16 : 18.
[4] Jn. 21 : 25. [5] Apoc. 10 : 3f. [6] Cf. no. 73 *supra*.

EUSEBIUS

98

a But since we have reached this point, it is reasonable to sum up the said writings of the New Testament. Indeed, the holy quaternion of the Gospels must be arranged among the first [books] which the book of The Acts of the Apostles follows. After this [book] the Epistles of Paul must be enumerated, following which the extant former Epistle of John and likewise the Epistle of Peter must be pronounced authoritative. To these must be added, if it would seem [permissible], the Apocalypse of John, the opinions regarding which we shall expound in due time. These, then, are among the accepted [writings]. But of the disputed, nevertheless known to the people, there are in circulation the so-called [Epistles] of James, and Jude, and the second Epistle of Peter and the so-named second and third [Epistles] of John, whether they happen to be of the Evangelist or even of
b another [author] of the same name as he. Among the spurious must be placed also the book of The Acts of Paul, both the

Canon

Ἀποκάλυψις Πέτρου καὶ πρὸς τούτοις ἡ φερομένη Βαρναβᾶ ἐπιστολὴ καὶ τῶν ἀποστόλων αἱ λεγόμεναι Διδαχαὶ ἔτι τε, ὡς ἔφην, ἡ Ἰωάννου Ἀποκάλυψις, εἰ φανείη· ἥν τινες, ὡς ἔφην, ἀθετοῦσιν, ἕτεροι δὲ ἐγκρίνουσιν τοῖς ὁμολογουμένοις. ἤδη δ' ἐν τούτοις τινὲς καὶ τὸ καθ' Ἑβραίους εὐαγγέλιον κατέλεξαν, ᾧ μάλιστα Ἑβραίων οἱ τὸν Χριστὸν παραδεξάμενοι χαίρουσιν. ταῦτα δὲ πάντα τῶν ἀντιλεγομένων ἂν εἴη, ἀναγκαίως δὲ καὶ τούτων ὅμως τὸν κατάλογον πεποιήμεθα, διακρίνοντες τάς τε κατὰ τὴν ἐκκλησιαστικὴν παράδοσιν ἀληθεῖς καὶ ἀπλάστους καὶ ἀνωμολογημένας γραφὰς καὶ τὰς ἄλλως παρὰ ταύτας, οὐκ ἐνδιαθήκους μὲν ἀλλὰ καὶ ἀντιλεγομένας, ὅμως δὲ παρὰ πλείστοις τῶν ἐκκλησιαστικῶν γινωσκομένας, ἵν' εἰδέναι ἔχοιμεν αὐτάς τε ταύτας καὶ τὰς ὀνόματι τῶν ἀποστόλων πρὸς τῶν αἱρετικῶν προφερομένας ἤτοι ὡς Πέτρου καὶ Θωμᾶ καὶ Ματθία ἢ καί τινων παρὰ τούτους ἄλλων εὐαγγέλια περιεχούσας ἢ ὡς Ἀνδρέου καὶ Ἰωάννου καὶ τῶν ἄλλων ἀποστόλων πράξεις· ὧν οὐδὲν οὐδαμῶς ἐν συγγράμματι τῶν κατὰ τὰς διαδοχὰς ἐκκλησιαστικῶν τις ἀνὴρ εἰς μνήμην ἀγαγεῖν ἠξίωσεν, πόρρω δέ που καὶ ὁ τῆς φράσεως παρὰ τὸ ἦθος τὸ ἀποστολικὸν ἐναλλάττει χαρακτήρ, ἥ τε γνώμη καὶ ἡ τῶν ἐν αὐτοῖς φερομένων προαίρεσις πλεῖστον ὅσον τῆς ἀληθοῦς ὀρθοδοξίας ἀπᾴδουσα, ὅτι δὴ αἱρετικῶν ἀνδρῶν ἀναπλάσματα τυγχάνει, σαφῶς παρίστησιν· ὅθεν οὐδ' ἐν νόθοις αὐτὰ κατατακτέον, ἀλλ' ὡς ἄτοπα πάντῃ καὶ δυσσεβῆ παραιτητέον.

Eusebius *H.E.* III.25.

Cyrillus Hierosolymitanus

99

Τῆς δὲ καινῆς διαθήκης τὰ τέσσαρα μόνα εὐαγγέλια· τὰ δὲ λοιπὰ ψευδεπίγραφα καὶ βλαβερὰ τυγχάνει· ἔγραψαν καὶ Μανιχαῖοι κατὰ Θωμᾶν εὐαγγέλιον, ὅπερ, εὐωδίᾳ τῆς εὐαγγελικῆς ἐπωνυμίας ἐπικεχρωσμένον διαφθείρει τὰς ψυχὰς τῶν ἁπλουστέρων. δέχου δὲ καὶ τὰς Πράξεις τῶν δώδεκα ἀποστόλων· πρὸς τούτοις τὰς ἑπτὰ [τὴν] Ἰακώβου, καὶ [τὰς δύο] Πέτρου καὶ [τὰς τρεῖς] Ἰωάννου καὶ [τὴν] Ἰούδα καθολικὰς ἐπιστολάς· ἐπισφάγισμα δὲ τῶν πάντων, καὶ μαθητῶν τὸ τελευταῖον τὰς Παύλου δεκατέσσαρας ἐπιστολάς. τὰ δὲ λοιπὰ πάντα ἐν δευτέρῳ κείσθω. καὶ ὅσα ἐν ἐκκλησίᾳ μὴ ἀναγινώσκεται, ταῦτα μηδὲ κατὰ σεαυτὸν ἀναγίνωσκε, καθὼς ἤκουσας. καὶ τὰ μὲν περὶ τούτων ταῦτα.

Cyrillus *Catecheses* IV.36.

so called Shepherd and The Apocalypse of Peter, and in addition to these, the extant Epistle of Barnabas and the so-called Teachings of the Apostles and in addition, as I have said, the Apocalypse of John, it if would seem [permissible], which, as I have said, some reject, but others reckon among the accepted. And among these some have already enumerated even The Gospel according to the Hebrews, in which mainly such Hebrews as received Christ rejoice. All these would be among the disputed [writings], but nevertheless of necessity we have made a catalogue of these also, distinguishing the writings which, according to the ecclesiastical tradition, were acknowledged as both true and genuine, from the "others," beside these, not in the canon, which although even disputed, are yet recognized " by " most churchmen, in order that we should be able to know these same [writings] and those produced by the heretics indeed in the name of the Apostles, as if containing the Gospels of Peter and Thomas and Matthias, or beside these, even of some others, or [as if containing] the Acts of Andrew and John and of the other Apostles; none of which anyone of successive [generations] of churchmen ever deemed worthy of mention in a treatise. Their nature of diction, however, is also far different from the apostolic custom and their thought and choice of the material is so absolutely out of harmony with true orthodoxy, that they confirm " very " clearly that they are forgeries of heretical men. For this reason they must not even be placed among the spurious [writings], but must be denounced as altogether foul and impious.

CYRIL OF JERUSALEM (A. D. 315-386)

99

But the four Gospels alone belong to the New Testament; the rest happens to be pseudepigrapha and harmful. The Manicheans also wrote [The] Gospel according to Thomas, which indeed, having been camouflaged by the sweetness of its title derived from an evangelist, corrupts the souls of the simpler ones. But accept also the Acts of the twelve Apostles. In addition to these [accept] the seven Catholic Epistles: [the one] of James and [the two] of Peter and [the three] of John and [the one] of Jude; and accept lastly as the seal of all, even of the disciples, the fourteen Epistles of Paul. Let all the rest, however, be placed in secondary [rank]. And those which are not read in the Church, do not even read them privately as you have heard. " So much " then about these.

Athanasius

100

Τὰ δὲ τῆς καινῆς, πάλιν οὐκ ὀκνητέον εἰπεῖν· ἔστι γὰρ ταῦτα· εὐαγγέλια τέσσαρα κατὰ Ματθαῖον, κατὰ Μάρκον, κατὰ Λουκᾶν καὶ κατὰ Ἰωάννην. εἶτα [καὶ] μετὰ ταῦτα Πράξεις ἀποστόλων καὶ Ἐπιστολαὶ καθολικαὶ καλούμεναι τῶν ἀποστόλων ἑπτὰ οὕτως· Ἰακώβου μὲν μία, Πέτρου δὲ δύο, εἶτα Ἰωάννου τρεῖς καὶ μετὰ ταύτας Ἰούδα μία. πρὸς τούτοις Παύλου ἀποστόλου εἰσὶν ἐπιστολαὶ δεκατέσσαρες, τῇ τάξει γραφόμεναι οὕτως· πρώτη πρὸς Ῥωμαίους, εἶτα πρὸς Κορινθίους δύο, καὶ μετὰ ταύτας πρὸς Γαλάτας καὶ ἑξῆς πρὸς Ἐφεσίους, εἶτα πρὸς Φιλιππησίους καὶ πρὸς Κολοσσαεῖς καὶ πρὸς Θεσσαλονικεῖς δύο καὶ ἡ πρὸς Ἑβραίους. καὶ ἑξῆς πρὸς μὲν Τιμόθεον δύο, πρὸς δὲ Τίτον μία καὶ τελευταία ἡ πρὸς Φιλήμονα μία· καὶ πάλιν Ἰωάννου Ἀποκάλυψις. . . .

Ἀλλ' ἕνεκά γε πλείονος ἀκριβείας προστίθημι καὶ τοῦτο, γράφων ἀναγκαίως ὡς [ὅτι] ἐστὶ καὶ ἕτερα βιβλία τούτων ἔξωθεν, οὐ κανονιζόμενα μέν, τετυπωμένα δὲ παρὰ τῶν πατέρων ἀναγινώσκεσθαι τοῖς ἄρτι προσερχομένοις καὶ βουλομένοις κατηχεῖσθαι τὸν τῆς εὐσεβείας λόγον· Σοφία Σολομῶντος καὶ Σοφία Σιρὰχ καὶ Ἐσθὴρ καὶ Ἰουδὶθ καὶ Τωβίας καὶ Διδαχὴ καλουμένη τῶν ἀποστόλων καὶ ὁ Ποιμήν. καὶ ὅμως, ἀγαπητοί, κἀκείνων κανονιζομένων καὶ τούτων ἀναγινωσκομένων, οὐδαμοῦ τῶν ἀποκρύφων μνήμη, ἀλλὰ αἱρετικῶν ἐστιν ἐπίνοια, γραφόντων μὲν ὅτε θέλουσιν αὐτά, χαριζομένων δὲ καὶ προστιθέντων αὐτοῖς χρόνους, ἵνα ὡς παλαιὰ προφέροντες πρόφασιν ἔχωσιν ἀπατᾶν ἐκ τούτων τοὺς ἀκεραίους.

Athanasius *Epistola* XXXIX.7-9 et 11-12.

Epiphanius

101

Εἰ γὰρ ἦς ἐξ ἁγίου πνεύματος γεγεννημένος, καὶ προφήταις, καὶ ἀποστόλοις μεμαθητευμένος, ἔδει σε διελθόντα ἀπ' ἀρχῆς γενέσεως κόσμου ἄχρι τῶν τῆς Αἰσθὴρ χρόνων, ἐν εἴκοσι καὶ ἑπτὰ βίβλοις παλαιᾶς διαθήκης, εἴκοσι δύο ἀριθμουμένοις, τέτταρσι δὲ ἁγίοις εὐαγγελίοις, καὶ ἐν τεσσαρσικαίδεκα ἐπιστολαῖς τοῦ ἁγίου ἀποστόλου Παύλου, καὶ ἐν ταῖς πρὸ τούτων καὶ σὺν ταῖς ἐν τοῖς

ATHANASIUS (✠A. D. 373)[1]

100

There must be no hesitation to state again the [books] of the New Testament; for they are these: Four Gospels: according to Matthew, according to Mark, according to Luke, and according to John. Further, after these, also [The] Acts of [the] Apostles, and the seven so-called Catholic Epistles of the Apostles, as follows: One of James, but two of Peter, then, three of John, and after these, one of Jude. In addition to these there are fourteen Epistles of the Apostle Paul put down in the following order: The first to the Romans, then two to the Corinthians, and after these, [the Epistles] to the Galatians, and then to the Ephesians; further, [the Epistles] to the Philippians and to the Colossians and two to the Thessalonians, and the [Epistle] to the Hebrews. And next two [letters] to Timothy, but one to Titus, and the the last [being] the one to Philemon. Moreover, also the Apocalypse of John . . . .

But, writing of necessity, I add this for the sake of more completeness at least, that there are other books beside these, which although not canonized, were "recommended" by the Fathers to be read by[2] the novices and by those who desire to be instructed in the learning of piety: The Wisdom of Solomon, and the Wisdom of Sirach, and Esther, and Judith, and Tobit, and the so-called Teaching of the Apostles, and The Shepherd. And, beloved, the former being canonized and the latter being read, nevertheless there is no mention of the apocrypha, but they are a device of the heretics, [who], writing them when they desire, approve them and assign [early] dates to them so that, presenting [them] as ancient, they may have a pretence to lead astray the simple by these [writings].

[1] Athanasius wrote this 39th *Easter Letter* in A. D. 367. [2] Or "to the novices."

EPIPHANIUS (c. A. D. 315–403)

101

For if you had been begotten of the Holy Spirit, and had been instructed by prophets and Apostles, it would have been imperative that you—after you had gone through [the story] from the beginning of the "Genesis" of the world until the times of Esther [as contained] in twenty-seven books of the Old Testament, counted as twenty-two, also in the four holy Gospels, and in the fourteen Epistles of the holy Apostle Paul, and in the

αὐτῶν χρόνοις Πράξεσι τῶν Ἀποστόλων, Καθολικαῖς Ἐπιστολαῖς Ἰακώβου καὶ Πέτρου καὶ Ἰωάννου καὶ Ἰούδα, καὶ ἐν τῇ τοῦ Ἰωάννου Ἀποκαλύψει, ἔν τε ταῖς Σοφίας, Σολομῶντος τέ φημι, καὶ υἱοῦ Σιράχ, καὶ πάσαις ἁπλῶς γραφαῖς θείαις, καὶ ἑαυτοῦ καταγνῶναι, ὅτι ὄνομα, ὅπερ οὐδαμοῦ ἐντέτακται, [×ἦλθες ἡμῖν φέρων×,] οὐκ ἀπρεπὲς μὲν θεῷ, ἀλλ' εὐσεβὲς εἰς θεόν, τὸ τοῦ ἀγεννήτου ὄνομα, μηδαμοῦ δὲ ἐν θειᾷ γραφῇ ῥηθέν.

Epiphanius *Adu. Haereses* III.I.LXXVI.5.

Canon Mommsenianus

102

Sed ut in apocalypsi Iohannis dictum est Uidi XXIIII se/niores mittentes coronas suas ante thronum. maiores nostri probant, hos libros esse canonicos et hoc dixisse seniores.

Item indiculum noui testamenti

Euangelia IIII	Mattheum	u̅r̅ I̅I̅DCC
	Marcum	u̅e̅r̅ MDCC
	Iohannem	u̅r̅ MDCCC
	Lucam	u̅r̅ I̅I̅I̅CCC
Fiunt omnes		uersus X
Eplae Pauli		n̅ XIII
Actus aplorum		u̅e̅r̅ I̅I̅I̅DC
Apocalipsis		u̅e̅r̅ MDCCC
Eplae Iohannis III		u̅r̅ CCCL
[una sola]		
Eplae Petri II		u̅e̅r̅ CCC
[una sola]		

Erwin Preuschen, *op. cit.*, p. 37.

Catholic Epistles of James and Peter and John and Jude, before[1] these [Epistles of Paul] and with the Acts of the Apostles, which is simultaneously with [the Epistles of Paul],[2] and in the Apocalypse of John, and in the Wisdom Literature, I mean both of Solomon and of the son of Sirach, and in short, in all the divine writings—judge of your own accord that [a book] whose name is nowhere listed [ˣyou come to us bringingˣ] is not unfitting to God, but pious toward God, but the name of the spurious [book] has not been mentioned anywhere in Holy Scripture.

[1] Before in a chronological sense, or in arrangement.
[2] The Latin rendering of Migne, *Epiphanius* II, p. 560, reads: "... *Pauli XIV Epistolis, necnon et Apostolorum Actis, quae vel superiora illis tempora, vel posteriora continent; catholicis item Epistolis, Jacobi, Petri*...."

THE CANON OF MOMMSEN (c. early 4th cent.)

102

But as it is said in the Apocalypse of John: "I saw twenty-four elders presenting their crowns before the throne," [so] our fathers approved that these books are canonical and that the men of old have said this:

The content of the New Testament, then, is:

The four Gospels: Matthew—2,700 lines,[1]
                    Mark —1,700 lines,
                    John —1,800 lines,
                    Luke —3,300 lines;

All "totaling" 10,000 lines;
The Epistles of Paul, thirteen in number;
The Acts of the Apostles—3,600 lines;
The Apocalypse—1,800 lines;
Three Epistles of John—350 lines;
  [one only];
Two Epistles of Peter—300 lines,
  [one only].

[1] "Versus" may mean as much as could be said in one breath.

Codex Claromontanus
104
Uersus scribturarum sanctarum ita ..

Euangelia IIII
Mattheum uer. ĪIDC
Iohannes uer. ĪI
Marcus uer. ĪDC
Lucam uer. ĪIDCCCC
Epistulas Pauli
ad Romanos uer. ĪXL
ad Chorintios I uer. ĪLX
ad Chorintios II uer LXX
ad Galatas uer. CCCL
ad Efesios uer. CCCLXXV
ad Timotheum I uer. CCVIII
ad Timotheum II uer. CCLXXXVIIII
ad Titum uer. CXL
ad Colosenses uer. CCLI
ad Filimonem uer. L
ad Petrum prima CC
ad Petrum II uer. CXL
Iacobi uer. CCXX
Pr. Iohanni epist. CCXX
Iohanni epistula II XX
Iohanni epistula III XX
Iudae epistula uer. LX
Barnabae epist. uer. DCCCL
Iohannis reuelatio ĪCC
Actus apostolorum ĪIDC
Pastoris uersi ĪIII
Actus Pauli uer. ĪIIDLX
Reuelatio Petri CCLXX.

Erwin Preuschen, *op. cit.*, pp. 40–42.

CODEX SINAITICUS (c. A.D. 350)

103

Matthew, Mark, Luke, John, Romans, Corinthians two [epistles], Galatians, Ephesians, Philippians, Colossians, Thessalonians two [epistles], Hebrews, Timothy two [letters], Titus, Philemon, Acts, James, Peter two [epistles], John three [epistles], Apocalypse, *Barnabas*, *Shepherd of Hermas*.

CODEX CLAROMONTANUS (c. 6th century)

104

The lines of the Holy Scriptures are as follows: ...
The four Gospels:
Matthew—2,600 lines,
John —2,000 lines,
Mark —1,600 lines,
Luke —2,900 lines;
The Epistles of Paul:
To the Romans—1,040 lines,
To the Corinthians, the first [epistle]—1,060 lines,
To the Corinthians, the second [epistle]—70 lines,
To the Galatians—350 lines,
To the Ephesians—375 lines,
To Timothy, the first [epistle]—208 lines,
To Timothy, the second [epistle]—289 lines,
To Titus—140 lines,
To the Colossians—251 lines,
To Philemon—50 lines,
The first [epistle] according to Peter—200 lines.
The second [epistle] according to Peter—140 lines.
James—220 lines
The first epistle of John—220 lines,
The second epistle of John—20 lines,
The third epistle of John—20 lines,
The epistle of Jude—60 lines,
The epistle of Barnabas—850 lines,
The Revelation of John—1,200 lines,
The Acts of the Apostles—2,600 lines,
Of The Shepherd [of Hermas]—4,000 lines,
The Acts of Paul—3,560 lines,
The Revelation of Peter—270 lines.

Canon Synodi Laodiciae
105

Ὅτι οὐ δεῖ ἰδιωτικοὺς ψαλμοὺς λέγεσθαι ἐν τῇ ἐκκλησίᾳ, οὐδὲ ἀκανόνιστα βιβλία, ἀλλὰ μόνα τὰ κανονικὰ τῆς καινῆς καὶ παλαιᾶς διαθήκης. Ὅσα δεῖ βιβλία ἀναγινώσκεσθαι· . . .
[Τὰ δὲ τῆς] καινῆς διαθήκης [ταῦτα]·
Εὐαγγέλια δ'·
κατὰ Ματθαῖον,
κατὰ Μάρκον,
κατὰ Λουκᾶν,
κατὰ Ἰωάννην.
Πράξεις Ἀποστόλων.
Ἐπιστολαὶ Καθολικαὶ ἑπτά· οὕτως
Ἰακώβου α'.
Πέτρου α'. β'.
Ἰωάννου α'. β'. γ'
Ἰούδα α'.
Ἐπιστολαὶ Παύλου ιδ'.
πρὸς Ῥωμαίους α'.
πρὸς Κορινθίους α'. β'.
πρὸς Γαλάτας α'.
πρὸς Ἐφεσίους α'.
πρὸς Φιλιππησίους α'.
πρὸς Κολοσσαεῖς α'.
πρὸς Θεσσαλονικεῖς α'. β'.
πρὸς Ἑβραίους α'.
πρὸς Τιμόθεον α'. β'.
πρὸς Τίτον α'.
πρὸς Φιλήμονα α'.

Erwin Preuschen, *op. cit.*, pp. 70 sq.

THE CANON OF THE SYNOD OF LAODICEA
(A. D. 360)
105

[Canon 59. It is decreed] that private psalms should not be read in the Church, neither uncanonized books, but only the canonical [books] of the New and Old Testament. [60] The books which should be read: ...

[And these] of [the] New Testament:
Four Gospels:
  According to Matthew,
  According to Mark,
  According to Luke,
  According to John.
The Acts of the Apostles.
The seven Catholic Epistles as follows:
  One of James,
  First [and] second of Peter,
  First, second, [and] third of John,
  One of Jude.
Fourteen epistles of Paul:
  To the Romans one [epistle],
  To the Corinthians a first [and] a second [epistle],
  To the Galatians one,
  To the Ephesians one,
  To the Philippians one,
  To the Colossians one,
  To the Thessalonians a first [and] a second [epistle],
  To the Hebrews one,
  To Timothy a first [and] a second [epistle],
  To Titus one,
  To Philemon one.

Canon Synodi Carthaginis
106

Item placuit, ut praeter scripturas canonicas nihil in ecclesia legatur sub nomine diuinarum scripturarum. sunt autem canonicae scripturae hae: ...

    Noui autem Testamenti
        Euangeliorum libri quattuor,
        Actuum apostolorum liber unus,
        Epistulae Pauli apostoli tredecim,
        eiusdem ad Hebraeos una,
        Petri apostoli duae,
        Iohannis tres,
        Iacobi una
        Iudae una
        Apocalypsis Iohannis liber unus.

... Liceat autem legi passiones martyrum cum anniuersarii eorum dies celebrantur.

Erwin Preuschen, *op. cit.*, pp. 72 sq.

THE CANON OF THE SYNOD OF CARTHAGE
(A.D. 397)
106

[Canon 47]. And so it seemed good that nothing should be read in the Church under the name of the Divine Scriptures except the canonical writings. The canonical writings, then, are these: . . .
and of the New Testament:
The four books of the Gospels,
The one book of the Acts of the Apostles,
The thirteen Epistles of the Apostle Paul,
Of the same [author] one [Epistle] to the Hebrews,
Two [Epistles] of the Apostle Peter,
Three of John
One of James,
One of Jude,
The Apocalypse of John—one book.
. . . Let it be permitted, however, that the passions of martyrs be read when their anniversaries are celebrated.

APPENDICES

I. Roman Emperors

Julius Caesar ✠ Mar. 15, 44 B. C.
Augustus Jan., 27 B. C. – A. D. Aug. 19, 14.
Tiberius A. D. 14 – Mar. 16, 37.
Caligula A. D. 37 – Jan. 24, 41.
Claudius A. D. 41 – Oct. 13, 54.
Nero A. D. 54 – June 9, 68.
Galba, Otho, Vitellius A. D. 68 – 69.
Vespasian A. D. July 1, 69 – June 23, 79.
Titus A. D. 79 – Sept. 13, 81.
Domitian A.D. 81 – Sept. 18, 96.
Nerva A. D. 96 – Jan. 27, 98.
Trajan A. D. 98 – Aug. 9, 117.
Hadrian A. D. 117 – July 10, 138.

II. Legatees of Syria

	Mommsen	Ramsay
M. Titius	9 B. C.	9 B. C.
C. S. Saturninus	8 B. C.	9–7 B. C.
P. Q. Varus	6–4 B. C.	7–4 B. C.
P. S. Quirinus	3–2 B. C.	7–4 B. C.
L. V. Saturninus	4 B. C. – A. D. 5	4 B. C. – A. D. 5
P. S. Quirinius	A. D. 6	A. D. 6

III. Procurators of Palestine

JUDEA, SAMARIA, IDUMEA

Conopius A. D. 6.
M. Ambivius A. D. 10.
Annius Rufus A. D. 13.
Valerius Gratus A. D. 15–26.
Pontius Pilate A. D. 26–35 (36).
Marcellus A. D. 35 (36).
Maryllus A. D. 38–41.

III. Procurators of Palestine *(contd.)*
PALESTINE

Cuspius Fadus A. D. 44–46
Tiberius Alexander A. D. 46–48.
Ventidius Cumanus A. D. 48.
Felix A. D. 52.
Porcius Festus A. D. 60 (56?)–62.
Albinus A. D. 62–64.
Gessius Florus A. D. 65–66.
(War with Rome A. D. 66.
Fall of Jerusalem (Titus) A. D. Sept. 70.
War with Rome under Hadrian A. D. 132–135).

IV. The Herodians

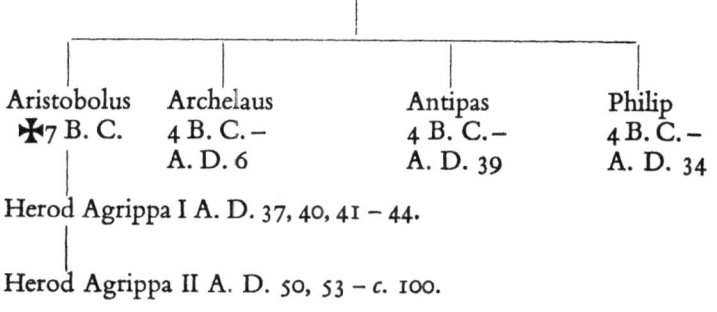

Herod Agrippa I A. D. 37, 40, 41 – 44.

Herod Agrippa II A. D. 50, 53 – *c.* 100.

V. Early Authors and Literature

Clement of Rome to the Corinthians—I Clement —, Rome, *c.* A. D. 96.
Clement of Rome to the Corinthians—II Clement (spurious)— Italy, *c.* A. D. 120–150.
Barnabas, Egypt, *c.* A. D. 100–130.
Hermas, Italy, *c.* A. D. 100–145.
Ignatius, Antioch, *c.* A. D. 100–117.
Polycarp, Smyrna, *c.* A. D. 115.
(Martyrdom of Polycarp A. D. 155).
Didache *c.* A. D. 100–130.
Gospel according to the Hebrews *c.* A. D. 120–130.
Gospel of Peter *c.* A. D. 120–140.
Papias, Hierapolis, *c.* A. D. 130–140.

V. Early Authors and Literature *(contd.)*

Gospel according to the Egyptians c. A. D. 130–140.
Marcion, Rome, c. A. D. 140.
Justin, Rome, c. A. D. 110–165.
Tatian, Rome, c. A. D. 160.
Acts of Paul c. A. D. 160.
Theophilus, Antioch, c. A. D. 170–180.
Polycrates, Ephesus, c. A. D. 190.
Canon of Muratori, Italy (?), c. A. D. 170–190
Irenaeus, Lyons, c. A. D. 125/140–200.
Gospel of the Ebionites c. A. D. 185 (?).
Pantaenus, Alexandria, c. A. D. 180.
Clement, Alexandria, c. A. D. 150–203.
Tertullian, Carthage, c. A. D. 155–222.
Acts of Peter c. A. D. 200.
Hippolytus, Rome, c. A. D. 170–236.
Origen, Alexandria, c. A. D. 182/186–251/254).
Letter of Abgar c. A. D. 250.
Gaius, Rome c. A. D. 283–296.
Eusebius, Caesarea, c. A. D. 270–340.
Eusebius, C. H., A. D. 324/325.
Athanasius, Alexandria, c. A. D. 296–373.
Athanasius, 39th *Easter Letter*, A. D. 367.
Cyril of Jerusalem, A. D. 315–386
Jerome, A. D. 340–420.
Epiphanius, Salamis, c. A. D. 315–403.
Augustin, North Africa and Italy, A. D. 354–430.
The Canon of Mommsen c. early 4th cent.
The Canon of the Synod of Laodicea A. D. 360.
The Canon of the Synod of Carthage A. D. 397.

INDEX

Abgar, 15
Achaea, 14, 38, 43a
Achaeans, 59
Acts (of the Apostles), 43b, 50, 51a, b, 57, 72, 73, 93, 96c, 98a, 100, 101, 102, 103, 104, 105, 106
Aenon near Salim, 34c
Agrapha, 82–88
Albinus, 2, 2 no.2
Alexandria, 37, 44b, 49
Alexandrians, 96d
Almighty, 72
Alphaeus, 89d
Amyntas, 13
Ananus, 2
Andrew, 18b, 51b, 89d, 96a
Andrew (Acts of), 98c
Annianus, 49
Antichrists, 39
Antioch, 38, 43a, 50, 51a
Apelles, 35a
Apocalypse (cf. Revelation), 18c. 19 no.1, 42b, 77, 96d, e, 97b, 98a, b, 100, 101, 102, 103, 106
Apollo, 14
Apostle(s), 17a, 18b, c, 19, 20, 21, 24, 27, 30a, 32, 34d, 35a, 37, 38, 39, 41b, 43a, b, 46, 47, 50, 51a, b, 54a, 58, 59, 61, 62, 63, 64, 65, 72, 73, 74, 77, 78, 91, 92, 93, "94," 96a, e, 97b, 98b, c, 99, 100, 101, 106.
Archippus, 64
Aretas King of the Nabateans, 3 no.2

Aristion, 18b, c, 19
Ark of the Covenant, 35b
Arsinoes, 96e
Asia, 10 no.1, 13, 16, 17a, 20, 21, 30b, 39, 42b, 51b, 54a, b
Asians, 62, 64
Athanasius, 100
Athenians, 12
Athens, 57, 65, 66
Augustin, 40
Augustus, 13, Ap. I
Babylon, 49, 78, 97a
Barnabas, 74, 75
Barnabas (Epistle of), 71, 74, 76, 98, 103, 104
Bartholomew, 35a, 46
Basilides, 35a, 96e
Bithynia, 43a
Boeotia, 38
Caesarea, 91
Canon of Mommsen, 102
Canun, 24
Carthage (Synod of), 106
Cataphrygians of Asia, 96e (?)
Catholic Epistles, 75, 76, 97a, 99, 100, 101, 105
Cerinthus, 27, 39, 53, 54a
Chaldee, 91
Chrestus, 7
Christ, 1, 2, 4, 6, 9c, 20, 27, 30, b, 32, 34a, c, 39, 40a, 41a, b, 42a, b, 43b, 44a, 46, 49, 53, 54a, 58, 65, 77, 79, 90, 96a, c, 97a, b, 98b
Christian, 9a, e
Christianity, 9a
Christians, 1, 6, 8, 9a, b, c, e, 10

131

Church, 17a, 30b, 35b, 95, 96d, e, 97a, b, 99, 105, 106
Claudius, 14, Ap. I
Clement of Alexandria, 31, 49, 57, 71, 75
Clement of Rome, 25, 71
Codex Claromontanus, 104
Codex Sinaiticus, 103
Colossians (Epistle to the), 64, 96d, 100, 103, 104, 105
Colossians (people), 51a, 64
Constantine, 51a
Constantinople, 51b
Corinth, 58
I Corinthians, 59, 96c, d, 100, 103, 104, 105
II Corinthians, 60, 100, 103, 104, 105
Corinthians (people), 59
Creator, 53
Crete, 13
Cyprus, 56
Cyrene, 13
Cyril of Jerusalem, 99
Day (the Lord's), 89c
Day of Preparation, 29
Day of Unleavened Bread, 89d
De vita contemplativa (Philo), 49
Delphians, 14
Diatessaron (Tatian), 28, 29
Discussion (Gaius), 27
Domitian, 20, 54b, Ap. II
Ebion, 39
Ebionites, 54a
Ecclesiastical History (Eusebius), 39
Egypt, 49
Eyptians (Gospel of), 35a
Epaphroditus, 63
Ephesians (Epistle to the), 62, 96d, 100, 103, 104, 105
Ephesians (people), 62
Ephesus, 16, 18c, 20, 21, 30b, 42b, 54b, 59, 61, 64
Epictetus, 11
Epiphanius 101,
Esoterics (Papias), 22
Esther, 100, 101
Eusebius, 20, 34a, 50, 98a
Evangelist(s), 18b, 35a, 39, 42a, 44a, " 94 "
Exposition on the Gospel according to John (Origen), 97b.
Father, 20b, 41b, 52, 83
Festus, 2, Ap. IV
Florinus, 17a
Freer Logion, 79
Gaius, 54b
Gaius of Rome, 27
Galatians (Epistle to the), 61, 96c, 100, 103, 104, 105
Galatians (people), 13 2, 61, 93
Galileans, 11
Galilee, 34b
Gallio, 14
Genesis, 42b, " 101 "
Gentiles, 72, 97a
God, 3, 5a, 12, 17a, b, 27, 29, 30a, b, 32, 35b, 39, 41a, b, 42a, b, 43a, b, 44a, b, 52, 53, 73, 74, 79
Gospel(s), 20, 28, 30a, b, 31, 33, 34a, b, c, d, 35a, b, 36, 38, 41a, b, 42a, b, 43a, b, 44, 46, 47, 49, 50, 51a, 51b, 53, 54a, 56, 73, 80, 91, 93, 95, 96a, b, 97a, b, 98a, b, c, 99, 100, 101, 104, 105, 106
Serennius Granianus, 10
Greek(s), 1, 24, 40, 47, 51a, 61, 72, 73, 80, 93
Hadrian, 10, Ap. I
Hebrew(s), 30b, 36, 45, 46, 72, 97a

Index

Hebrews (Epistle to the), 71, 72, 73, 74, 97b, 100, 103, 105, 106
Hebrews (Gospel according to the), 90, 91, 92 no.1, 98b
Hercules, 10
Herod Agrippa II, 2 no.3
Herod Antipas, 3 no.1
Hierapolis, 19, 20, 21, 49
Hippolytus, 78
Homilies (Origen), 73, 97b
Homonadenses, 13
Illyricum, 97b
Irenaeus, 16, 17a, 18a, 30a, 53, 54b, 56, 94
Isaiah, 78
Israel, 44a
Italy, 44a, 58
James, 18b, 19, 24, 54a, 76
James, brother of Jesus, 2, 4, 93
James (Epistle of), 76, 98a, 99, 100, 101, 103, 104, 105, 106
Jerome, 35a, 47, 49, 51a, 53a, 80, 91
Jerusalem, 4, 15, 24, 27, 49, 77, 89a, 97b
Jesus, 1, 2, 3, 4, 5, 15, 29, 34b, c, 36, 39, 54a, 55, 58, 65, 80, 81, 82, 83, 84, 97a, b
Jesus Sirach, 71
Jewish, 49
Jewish books, 69
Jewish fables, 43a
Jewish law, 59
Jewish leaders, 5b
Jewish tribes, 5b
Jewish War (Josephus), 5a
Jews, 1, 3, 7, 12, 19, 20, 29, 36, 49, 55, 89b, c
John, 16, 17b, 18b, c, 19, 20, 21, 22, 24, 30b, 31, 32, 33, 34a, b, c, d, 35b, 39, 42a, b, 43b, 44a, 51b, 52, 53, 54a, 76, 77, 78, 96a, b, c, d, 97a, b, 98a, 100, 102, 103, 104, 105
John (Acts of), 98c
John the Baptist, 3, 4, 34a, b, c, 54a, 91
John the Evangelist, 54b, 98a
John the Presbyter, 54b
I John (cf. John), 98a, 99, 100, 101 (?), 102, 103, 104, 105, 106
II John (cf. John), 98a, 99, 100, 101 (?), 102, 103, 104, 105, 106
III John (cf. John), 98a, 99, 100, 101 (?), 102, 103, 104, 105, 106
Joseph (of Aramathea), 29, 89b
Josephus, 1, 2, 3, 4
Judaism, 97
Jude, 71, 75, 76, 96e, 98a, 99, 100, 104, 105, 106
Judea, 6, 29, 34b, 36, 41a, 43a, 47, 89a
Judith, 100
Juno, 12
Justin Martyr, 54b, 77
Laodicea (Synod of), 105
Laodiceans, 64, 96d
Latin, 93
Levi (cf. Matthew), 36, 47, 89d
Levite, 44a
Lord, 16, 17b, 18b, 19, 20, 21, 30a, b, 34a, 35b, 39, 40, 42a, b, 43a, b, 44a, b, 48, 51b, 53, 54a, b, 56, 58, 72, 78, 82, 86, 87, 88, 89 a, b, c, 93, 96a, b
Luke, 30b, 32, 33, 34b, c, d, 35a, 38, 40, 43a, b, 50a, 51a, b, 54a, 56, 57, 72, 73, 76, 96a, b, c, 97a, 100, 102, 103, 104, 105

Index

Lystra, 26
Macedonians, 63, 65
Machaerus, 3
Manichaeans, 99
Mara, 12
Marcion, 22, 96d, e
Marcionite Prologues, 58
Mark, 30b, 31, 32, 33, 34a, b, d, 37, 40, 43a, 44a, b, 44a, b, 48, 49, 54a, 56, 76, 96a, 97a, 100, 102, 103, 104, 105
Mary, 54a
Mary Magdalene, 89c
Matthew, 18b, 19, 32, 33, 34a, b, c, 35a, 36, 40, 41a, b, 42b, 43a, 45, 46, 47, 54a, 76, 91, 97a, 100, 102, 103, 104, 105
Matthias, 35a
Matthias (Gospel of), 98c
Metiades, 96c (?)
Miscellanies (71)
Monarchian Prologues, 41a
Mount of Olives, 5b
Muratorian Canon, 96a
Munucius Fundanus, 10
Nathan, 43b
Nazarenes, 91
Nero, 6, 51a, 54b, Ap. I
Nerva, 20, 54b, Ap. I
New Testament, 98a, 99, 100, 102, 105, 106
Nicolaitans, 54
Nicomedia, 24
Old Testament, 101, 105
Onesimus, 71
Onesiphorus, 26
Only-begotten, 53
Origen, 20, 23, 73, 90, 93, 97a
Outlines (Clemens Alexandrinus), 49, 75
Pantaenus of Alexandria, 46
Papias, 18a, c, 19, 20, 21, 48, 54b

Paradise, 35b
Parthia, 2a
Patmos, 23, 54b, 78
Paul, 16, 24, 25, 26, 30b, 33, 34d, 38, 39, 43a, b, 50, 51a, b, 56, 57, 58, 72, 73, 74, 76, 93, 96a, c, d, 97a, b, 98a, 99, 100, 101, 102, 104, 105, 106
Paul (Acts of), 98b, 104
Paul and Thecla (Acts of), 51a
Peter (cf. Simon, Cephas), 18b, 19, 30b, 31, 33, 37, 44a, 48, 49, 76, 81, 89d, 96c, 97b, 98a
Peter (Apocalypse of), 75, 96e, 98c
Peter (Gospel of), 89, 98b
Peter (Revelation of — cf. Apocalypse), 104
I Peter, 49, 98a, 99, 100, 101 (?), 102, 103, 104, 105, 106
II Peter, 98a, 99, 100, 101 (?), 102, 103, 104, 105, 106
Philemon, 70, 96d, 100, 103, 104, 105
Philip, 18b, 19
Philippians (Epistle to the), 63, 96d, 100, 103, 105
Philippians (people), 63
Philo, 49
Phoenicia, 13
Pilate, 1, 5c, 6, 55, 89c, Ap. III
Pius, 96e
Plato, 12
Pleroma, 53
Pliny, 9a, e
Polycarp, 17a, b, 18a, 19
Polycrates, 21
Pontus, 22
Presbyter, 48, 54b
Pythagoras, 12
Publius Quirinius, 13, Ap. II
Redeemer, 35b

Index

Revelation (cf. Apocalypse), 104
Roman hands, 5b
Roman troops, 5b
Romans (Epistle to the) 58, 96c, d, 100, 103, 104, 105
Romans (people), 5c, 13, 23, 58, 73
Rome, 7, 9b, 24, 30b, 31, 49, 51a, 62, 63, 70, 96e
John Rylands Library, 55
Sabbath, 29
Sadducee, 2 no.1
Salome, 29
Samians, 12
Samos, 12
Satan, 79, 80
Saviour, 34b, c, 37, 39, 90, 93
Scripture(s), 17b, 30a, 52, 96c, 104, 106
Serapion, 12
Shepherd (of Hermas), 74, 96e, 98b, 100, 103
Simon Cephas (cf. Peter), 24
Socrates, 12
Spain, 96c
Spirit (Holy), 21 30a, 31, 34c, 35b, 43a, 74, 90, 92, 95, 96b, 101
Stephen, 24
Suetonius, 7
Publius Sulpicius, 13
Syria, 13
Syriac language, 91
Syriac Martyrology, 24
Syrian, 38, 43a

Tacitus, 6
Tatian, 28
Tertullian, 32, 51b, 74
Theophilus, 52
Theophilus (most excellent), 96c
Thessalonians (people), 65, 66
I Thessalonians, 65, 96d, 100 103, 105
II Thessalonians, 66, 96d, 100, 103, 105
Thomas, 18b, 19, 20, 35a
Thomas (Gospel of), 98c, 99
Tiberius, 6
Timothy, 51a, 59, 67, 68, 96d
I Timothy, 67, 100, 103, 104, 105
II Timothy, 68, 100, 103, 104, 105
Titus, 26
Titus (Letter to), 69, 96d, 100, 103, 104, 105
Tobit, 100
Troas, 56, 60
Trajan, 9a, 16, 54b, Ap. I
Tychicus, 62
Valentinian, 17 no.1
Valentinus, 96e
Wisdom of Sirach (cf. Jesus Sirach), 100, 101
Wisdom of Solomon, 71, 96e, 100, 101
Word, 17b, 35a, 39, 42a, 44a, b, 53, 52, 90
Zacharias, 44a
Zebedee, 23, 29, 30

www.ingramcontent.com/pod-product-compliance
Lightning Source LLC
Chambersburg PA
CBHW070047100426
42734CB00039B/2137